This book is dedicated to my two daughters *Dorinda Akueku-Nimpah* and *Aimee Nimpah-Opoku*, whose patience and understanding provided me with the time and strength to string my ideas together.

CONTENTS

ACKNOWLEDGMENTS

To the Master of the Universe, I owe infinite gratitude. He/She/It was the source of inspiration. May this little book help to make the 'financial world' a better place to live in.

NOTE TO THE READER

HOW TO USE THIS BOOK

The topics in this book have been categorized into: *Personal finance, Investment, Insurance, Tax and Retirement planning*. The topics do not have to be read in the sequence they come in, as each of them is self-contained. You are thus welcome to choose the topics as your need dictates, and understanding will not be hindered.

SECTION A: PERSONAL FINANCE

What is Financial Planning All About?

It may seem a bit farfetched, but some investors have butterflies in the stomach when they hear about financial planning. There is no doubt that planning one's finances is a very necessary and beneficial practice, but what does the plan really entail? I feel strongly that a good answer can help to calm the fears of investors.

Financial planning basically involves making decisions in five main areas: budgeting, liquidity management, management of large purchases, long-term investment and insurance.

In budgeting, the investor is supposed to decide how much of his income will be saved and how much will be spent. When income exceeds expenditure, there is saving, and hence an increase in assets. When the reverse occurs, there is negative saving, or a rise in liabilities. The excess of assets over liabilities represents the net worth of the investor.

Saving broadly relates to three different time horizons. Short-term saving, such as saving for day to day expenses, has a connection with liquidity management which will soon be discussed. Medium-term management deals with saving for items such as a car, or deposit towards buying a house, and borders on financing large purchases. Long-term saving is needed to achieve long-term investment.

Liquidity stands for cash that can be readily spent. Generally speaking,

1

the more liquid a financial instrument is, the lower the returns it provides. Examples of very liquid instruments are bank notes, and current accounts. These instruments pay little or no interest. Bank and building society deposits are slightly less liquid instruments that pay some interest but with some amount of limitation in accessibility. Stock market securities such as shares and bonds provide much higher returns but are equally much less liquid. It is necessary for an investor to decide how much of his saving should be in very liquid form and otherwise, in order to maximise returns.

Some form of money management is needed. For example, the high dealing cost involved in the purchase and sales of shares will make it unreasonable to embark on a share investment when one is saving towards a holiday. A deposit or current account will be more suitable. Liquidity can also be maintained via the use of credit cards, except that this form of credit attracts high interest. One must decide how much liquidity will be provided by credit cards, through credit management.

When considering large purchases such as buying a car or house, one can use his own savings, borrow or combine both savings and borrowing. It pays to bear the interest as well as duration of repayment in mind when borrowing. Allowance should be made for possible hikes in interest, and a resultant rise in the size of the loan, and regular payments.

Returns increase more than proportionately with time, and risk increases less than proportionately with time when considering investment in shares. In other words, shares are more suitable for long-term investment than many other securities. There is time diversification which means that losses are evened out by gains with the passage of time. Another benefit of employing shares in long-term investments is their ability to nullify the negative effects of inflation. Shares have been proven to provide returns that are proportionately higher than inflation in the long-term.

Insurance is also considered in financial planning and essentially means paying money to an insurer for financial protection. Life insurance protects the beneficiaries in the event of the death of the policyholder. In fact insurance can be taken out to cover various assets such as car, property, and so on. It can provide protection against eventualities such as critical illness, sickness, income continuity following death and so on. Certain insurance policies such as endowment and whole-of-life combine both features of savings and life insurance in one package. It is wise to decide during planning whether it is better to keep savings and life insurance apart.

Financial planning should be demystified. It is like any other plan, except that it relates to finances. As long as one stays focused and methodical, and touches on the aforementioned decision zones there shouldn't be any anxieties. The plan is for a particular individual to use and it is crucial that decisions are made to suit the unique financial situation and circumstances of the person under consideration.

Brits Need to Step Up Their Savings

For some time, the UK state and occupational pension schemes have been sounding alarm bells, warning Brits about a relentless decline in future pensions. Many citizens appear to have turned a deaf ear to this message, and are still not saving enough to top-up future pensions. The sophisticated nature of the financial services industry, and turbulence in the stock market, among many other factors, have been blamed for the slow response.

The 11 September 2001 catastrophe dealt a very big blow to the already capricious stock market. Share prices fell, and when they were about to recover, the Enron and WorldCom scandals in late 2001 and early 2002 led to a further decline in prices. To add insult to injury, the war in Iraq and its cocktail of geopolitical events arrived. There is presently a lot of economic unrest world-wide, which is taking its toll on various stock markets, and leading to a further reluctance on the part of certain UK citizens to save and invest enough towards retirement.

Research carried out by the Consumers' Association around 2002 found that many Brits are not saving enough. In fact it was revealed that nearly 47 % were not saving towards their pensions and only 35 % felt they were saving amply towards their retirement. These figures are quite worrying considering that there is every sign that state pensions are going to get smaller and main UK employers have stopped offering final salary (defined benefit) pension schemes to their new employees, plus a cut of almost 30 % in contribution rates. There is a glaring indication that the load of providing for sufficient pension during retirement has been transferred from the state and employers, onto the shoulders of employees, and yet there hasn't been enough effort made to bear it.

Apart from recent fluctuations in the stock market, and perhaps lack of excess funds after expenditure, the reluctance to save has been put down to the complex nature of the financial services industry in UK and the lack of access to decent financial advice.

Child Trust is a good first step from the government to assist in the education of the citizens of the UK about savings. However, it looks as though the tutorial aspect of the programme can do with a lot of reinforcement. The essence of the scheme needs to be brought home to both parents and children; otherwise there will be a divergence from the attainment of its primary goals. The earlier the 'pension' problem is brought to the attention of children and teenagers the better it is. This can be a move in the right direction to uproot the delay and negligence that are normally displayed by most adults regarding retirement savings in the UK.

The panacea, it has been suggested, should be a simplification of financial products and the provision of affordable and unbiased financial advice that will be within an easy reach of all Brits. The entire pension system should be made a lot simpler and easy to understand and use. Indeed, it will take strenuous efforts from both government and citizens alike, to initiate a marked change. An overhaul of the whole financial services industry will be critical to motivate Brits to step up their savings towards retirement.

Watch the Birds and Build a Nest Egg for Your Future

Take a walk into the fields and watch a bird at work, building its nest. It is such a pretty sight. The bird travels far, picks a piece of straw in its beak, and darts back to the building site, tacks the straw in the right place and off it goes again. There is a splendid display of purpose, drive, will, tact and planning. Learn from these little creatures, and you can be successful in saving towards your dearest goals. You will be an expert in building a nest egg for your future.

A lot of people find it difficult to save because they lack a sense of purpose for the money they want to amass. I suppose you know the sort of situation you can get yourself into when you're bored at home and get out of your house to go for a walk without an exact place in mind you want to go to. You might even get lost with such lack of direction and destination. Sadly, most people who claim to be purposeful cannot tell you the definitive reasons why they are trying to save.

You can enhance your ability to save if you start by actually enlisting your purpose or purposes for saving, and proceed further to attach to each purpose specific goals. Goals serve as landmarks in your journey towards the purpose.

In order to set a realistic purpose it is crucial that you carry out a detailed assessment of the resources you presently have, and find out the extra resources you will need, to realize your purpose and its associated goals. The birds can really teach you to save. It becomes a lot easier once you establish a clear sense of purpose.

Time is of great essence when considering savings. The time for action is now; you must start now. You might already have an investment; the earlier you begin reviewing it the greater chances are that you will uncover any flaws and hopefully, rectify them before things really get out of hand. Remember the adages: 'A stitch in time saves nine' and 'make hay while the sun shines'. Believe it or not, time is the greatest enemy of mankind and has to be utilised resourcefully.

State pension and national insurance schemes have been in a shambles for a long time, and numerous occupational pension schemes are running deficits. You should be clear about the sort of retirement you want to experience. Would you like to maintain the same lifestyle you are enjoying now or even improve on it during retirement? Needless to say you must make allowance for the fact that sicknesses are rampant amongst the aged and that you may need to contribute massively towards care. You may have to commence saving towards a personal pension to top-up shortcomings in state and occupational pension.

Failing this, you may have to continue working during retirement, retire a lot later than you should, or live a life much below the standard you anticipate when you retire. I'll entreat you to give due attention to 'you' in the future, perhaps even more than you give to 'you' now, the reason being you are a lot stronger now than you will be then.

Everything, including savings can be achieved if you put your mind to it. Consider the size of ants and the gigantic hills they erect, and believe that you can save towards any purposes and goals. Why do you have to wait till the morrow? Start now, take your own future in your hands and make it brighter.

Long Term Saving is a Must

When income exceeds expenses, asset is created. When the reverse occurs debt or liability rises. The excess of income over expenditure can be saved with three time horizons in mind: short-term, medium-term and long-term. An example of short-term saving is the money one puts aside to take care of the following month's expenses before he gets paid. Saving towards a car can be considered as medium-term, whereas saving towards higher education of a toddler is long-term. Long-term saving can also be termed 'investment'. Short-term saving comes quite naturally to most of us, and with a bit of effort, medium-term saving does not become much of a hurdle to surmount. In spite of being the most important form of saving or investment, long-term saving is normally ignored.

Of all the long-term investments one can choose from, savings towards one's pension is crucial and should be a must. It does seem as though a host of people just can't be bothered to sit down to ponder the sort of lifestyle they want to live during retirement, and how to achieve it. Attitudes towards retirement have to change because statistical figures on demography, state and corporate provision seem pretty scary. Let's have a look.

Research by the US Census Bureau in 1999 revealed that in Western Europe the ratio of retirees (over sixty-five year olds) to those in employment in 1950 was 0.15. In 2000 this ratio was almost doubled, rising to 0.29. The research forecast that by 2050 this ratio will rise to about 0.64. We are talking about an increase from 1:6 in 1950 to a staggering 4:6 in 2050. This is the so called 'demographic time bomb'.

The relevant questions to ask here are: how is the state going to provide for this alarming jump in the number of retirees, when its pension and social security systems are crumbling? Will tax paid by the decreasing number of workers be enough to comfortably take care of the pensions of the rising number of retirees? Is it fair for the working group to part with their hard earned income to take care of retired people, considering that some were spendthrift during their working lives, and intentionally refused to save for their retirement? To make matters worse, a lot of occupational pension schemes are in deficits, with a concomitant denial of some retirees of the pensions they very much deserve.

Let us forget about the statistics for a moment and attempt to appreciate the reality of the situation from a basic arithmetic point of view. Assuming you start working at the age of twenty, retire at sixty and live for twenty years during retirement – assuming your lifespan is eighty years. If you decide to maintain your lifestyle as it is in the working time (forty years from age twenty to sixty) during your retirement, then you have to save a third of your earnings. Although net real rate of return on savings is not being considered here, to save a third of income will be quite daunting to many people. I'd like to draw your attention to the fact that in order to earn a pension of £20,000 a year, with an annuity rate of 8 %, one needs to have £250,000 sitting intact in a pension fund.

What is the way around this pension crisis, if one still wants to guarantee an easy retirement? Bank and building society deposits suit short-term time horizons, and besides, their returns are too meagre for this challenge. We have to consider a long-term investment with a good record of providing high returns in the long run.

Shares are a better fit than bonds in this respect, and provide a bonus of achieving returns that are proportionately higher than inflation rate. Lack of sufficient start funds should not be an excuse for not investing in shares, as one can commence investing indirectly on a small scale, by buying a stake in an investment trust, purchasing units in a unit trust or other OEICs.

There is nothing wrong with saving towards the attainment of short and medium-term goals. What is abominable is doing it at the expense of long-term savings, especially savings towards one's retirement. If the future will be worth looking forward to, it must be well planned and adequately prepared for.

Financial Planning Doesn't Hurt

A lot of people plan their day to day activities intent on working efficiently to earn high income. The irony is that when the expected income is obtained there isn't much thought given to how the income is spent, saved or invested. It is not as though these people have no medium and long-term financial objectives to reach. The select few who take the trouble to really put pen on paper to plan the use of their income, or in some cases employ the services of certified financial advisors enjoy great benefits. I can liken an effort to attain a medium/long-term goal without planning, to trying to fill an empty barrel sitting in your house with water from a pond, using a very porous bucket. You see you might succeed in filling the bucket, but it will be really tiring, and certainly not without causing a lot of mess on your floors!

The amount of uncertainty that is inherent in the future makes it necessary for one to make a lot of financial provision. It is necessary to stash some money away for emergencies. Allowance has to be made for a reserve to fall on when there is redundancy at work, as not all employers pay redundancy sums. Even if they do, the amount might not be enough to keep you and your family going before you resume work elsewhere. Not all employers provide sick pay, and those who do cover up to the first month or so. The big mistake many people commit is an over-reliance on state help; in practice, the latter does not materialise at all or comes in late and is normally quite inadequate. It is wise to have a minimum of six months' wages in savings to address any eventualities. Then there are the long-term financial needs of providing for education of children, mortgaging, and life insurance for family in the event of death, and so on to consider. I hope you see the point in financial planning from this angle.

By planning I do not mean a fussy construct of your expenditure, savings and investments in your mind. You will not benefit from inundating your brain with the complex and diverse information and factors that have to be considered to ensure an effective financial plan. A lot of factors such as the level of risk you can tolerate, the nature of your job, number of children, whether you are married or single, renting or having a mortgage, and many more have to be listed on paper, prioritised and looked at in detail, before arriving at a financial plan. Let me say in passing that you don't always need a financial advisor to plan your finances; you can learn to do it yourself. A financial advisor becomes necessary when you don't have the time to do it yourself or when extremely complex financial needs and instruments are under consideration.

The benefits of financial planning are almost obvious from the on-going discourse. It does lead to probing oneself to uncover ones personal circumstances and true financial needs, clarify financial objectives, and through in-depth research, secure the appropriate financial instruments whose benefits match the financial needs in question. Without doubt, it promotes focus and enhances the achievement of short, medium and long-term financial goals.

SECTION B: INVESTMENT

Issues That Create Top-Quality Investment Strategies

Let us assume there is something you have to get really badly. You don't know where to buy it from, but you've been lucky; a friend of yours knows somebody who has one to sell at a very low price. In fact, you have to be buying the product in person from time to time from the same seller. Your friend, who has to be flying to live abroad in a couple of hours' time, has offered to take you to the seller's house; you have to travel there alone next time. Can you imagine the effort you will make to register details of the route to the seller's house on your mind? You'll most likely be looking out for certain prominent objects on the way that will help jog your memory of the right direction next time you have to travel alone. Accordingly, when you want to arrive at a good investment strategy, there are certain relevant questions that have to be answered. These questions/issues are like the prominent objects on the way to the seller's house, and an omission of one of them is very likely to lead to a weak investment plan.

Change is a common phenomenon in the stock market, but age has always remained a very important issue to consider before choosing any financial product. For example, all things being equal, a person at the age of fifty-five will be more interested in saving enough for retirement than in saving towards a deposit to buy his first home.

A consideration of the investor's health is also of essence. An individual with a bad heart will find it difficult taking out life insurance or getting the

9

right amount of it. He might have to top-up the pension he will get with extra saving. Life insurance will favour a healthy investor much better.

Family matters also have to be considered. One may be considering how to save enough to build the right legacy to pass on to his offspring following death. It could also be savings to provide good quality higher education for children in the future.

It is also necessary to have a look at certain expectations. The investor may have to take note of an anticipated fall in income when he starts a family. On the flip side, he may be expecting a rise in salary when he acquires higher qualifications or after training, and may thus decide to run down his savings.

No matter what one does, one should not select any financial product without considering the suitability of his or her tax position. Certain investments will suit somebody with a high tax rate than a non-tax payer and vice versa.

Knowing what one wants from an investment is a matter of paramount importance. Is it an effort to build up enough pension for retirement? In this case the investor's focus will be income growth in the future. On the contrary, the investor might be in need of an investment that will supplement present income. It might even be an effort to build up some savings to pass on to the children.

One relevant question is: how much can the investor part with? Certain investments involve paying a lump sum, whereas others ask for regular monthly payments. Which of the two is the investor interested in and can afford?

Then there is this question: how long does the investor want to save for? Investments like shares have to be held for a minimum of five years (in fact ten years in the present climate), to provide returns higher than safer asset classes, such as gilts, bonds and bank deposits.

Ethical investments are now on the rise. It is necessary for the investor to have an idea about the range of products he/she might want to consider and those he/she might not want the funds invested in. For example, somebody might specify that he will not want an investment that deals in firearm production companies, or state a particular course towards which he will want his money to go.

In a nutshell, there are certain issues an investor has to ponder before investing. To recap, these are: age; health; family; expectations; tax position; what is wanted from the investment; how much can be invested; how long the investment will last; and the range of investments. It will take a lot of self-questioning to arrive at the right answers. The quality of the answers, of course, will depend on how honest one gets with himself. The success of the investment strategy will in turn depend on how genuine the answers are to the relevant questions asked.

How to Live With Risk in Saving

It is quite usual for some people who place their money with banks or building societies, for short-term saving purposes, to feel they are not operating under any risk. Short-term or long-term, the hard truth is that there is always an element of risk, even in bank deposits. The Financial Services Authority (FSA) is aware of this and is not aiming at creating zero risk, because it holds the view that it will hinder competition in the industry. If it is not possible to operate without risk, then it makes a lot of sense to find a way of controlling and containing the risk inherent in savings.

The select few who think there can be risk in saving normally consider the chances of being defrauded by a financial institution as the only risk. As an aside, by 'saving' our attention here is not on long-term investments such as shares, but on short-term products such as current accounts and bank deposits.

Risk related to savings can be divided into 'security' and 'unpredictability'. Security has to do with the possibility of losing the entire amount placed with the financial institution, whereas unpredictability concerns possible variations and uncertainty in the principal and its interest.

A most common security risk that a saver is exposed to is the probability of the financial institution going bust. This can result from general fraud in the institution or lack of financial control of staff who take undue risk with the institution's funds. Very typical recent examples of this are the BCCI and the Barings Bank cases.

This risk, however, does not often materialise due to efforts from the FSA. Banks, building societies, and other financial institutions in the UK have to be licensed by the FSA to take deposits from their clients. This requires them to hold a large amount of financial reserves in order to be able to satisfy withdrawal demands of their clients. If the worst happens and an authorised institution goes bust, a deposit protection scheme will compensate clients of the institution up to a limit of £85,000.

In order to control this risk the saver must first ensure that the bank or building society is authorised. Interestingly, smaller banks pay higher interest than bigger ones, but have a higher chance of going bust. There must be a trade-off between higher returns and peace of mind in this case.

It is also advisable to split savings higher than £85,000 amongst two or more banks. The irony is that putting the entire amount in the same account will normally provide a higher rate of return. There is again a choice between lower risk, and the possibility of earning higher returns by being more exposed to risk.

The unpredictability risk in a savings account has to do with the fact that interest rates of banks and building societies, depend on Bank of England's base rate, and vary very often. There is also uncertainty regarding the amount of money that will be collected at the end of the saving term due to the impact of inflation. Inflation can erode the purchasing power of both the principal and the interest it will amass.

The changes in the interest rates can be addressed by opting for a fixed interest account. Although the saver will be sitting fine on higher returns if interest rates on the market fall, he will also be stuck with a lower rate of interest, should interest rates on the market rise. A way around the bite of inflation is to place the fund in an index related savings account. These pay interest in line with movements in inflation.

Most of the risk associated with saving can be reduced to a bare minimum. It, nevertheless, often involves trading in higher risk for lower returns. The saver must thus decide what is more important: more returns or tranquillity of mind.

How to Live With Risk in Your Investment

Investment entails saving money with a long-term view in mind. It mainly involves dealings on the stock market. Broadly speaking, investors are exposed to two kinds of risk: 'specific' and 'unpredictability' risks. Unpredictability risk can be further divided into 'market' risk, 'currency' risk and 'manager' risk.

Specific risk is the probability that the company whose security money has been invested in will not perform well. For instance, if £12,000 is invested in the shares of a company, and the share price drops by 50 %, the investor will lose £6,000 of his investment. Specific risk can be the result of fraud or poor management in a company. Specific risk can be reduced by investing in a variety of companies. Another way of looking at it is making an effort not to 'put all of one's eggs in the same basket.' Thus if the same £12,000 mentioned above was instead invested in 6 different shares, placing £2,000 in each, a lot of the funds will be salvaged, if one company goes bust.

It must be noted that small companies have a higher tendency to go bust, and compensate for this by normally paying higher returns. It is advisable to buy securities only from legitimate and authorised firms.

Market risk is the probability that the market index as a whole will fall. When this happens the market normally drags the shares of the constituent companies with it. It is difficult for a company to totally buck movements in the market index.

Market risk can be reduced by investing in various stock markets around the globe as well as in different asset classes. This is because although trends in one stock market affect other international stock markets, the changes do not occur at the same time and will have different magnitudes. Movements in the prices of the different asset classes will also not take place at the same time, and will occur to varied extents. Buying units in a unit trust or shares in an investment trust are very efficient ways for the private investor to protect himself against market risk. This is because the pooled funds of these institutions are usually invested in a wide variety of assets, both domestically and internationally.

Currency risk is the risk that the value of an amount invested in a foreign country will fall when the income and principal are converted into the domestic currency. This will result from a fall in the domestic currency relative to the foreign currency. An investment in an international unit trust or investment trust will help to combat such a risk. A fall in the value of some of the currencies will be smoothed out by rises in others.

Manager risk has to do with the probability that the fund chosen will not perform as well as anticipated. History has shown that only one out of ten actively managed funds have consistently managed to outperform the stock index. Choosing a good fund manager, in practice, is not as simple as it sounds. Views of experts are divided between the possibility of predicting future performances from past ones. Index or tracker funds have proven to provide higher returns in the long-term than actively managed funds, and will be useful tools in controlling manager risk.

One golden rule of investment is that an investor should expect to take more risk if higher returns are expected. Another is that the longer the time-horizon an investor is prepared to accept for an investment, the greater his risk tolerance level. Risk is the fuel of an investment vehicle; there will be no investment without it. If it is properly harnessed and contained it can provide great returns, otherwise investment can go really awry.

How to Save and Invest Effectively

A host of saving and investment efforts fail to achieve their ends because of the use of wrong techniques. There are simple steps that can be followed to enhance saving and investment. A fervent dedication to the principles discussed below can provide better returns whilst guaranteeing the investor's peace of mind.

It is crucial to embrace the idea that investment is a long-term saving process. Every investment involves some amount of risk taking, and money can be lost irrespective of how perfect an investment strategy is. Hence one golden rule to bear in mind is: invest only what you can really afford to lose. I hope you can infer from this concept that before you start investing (putting money that might not come back to you somewhere), you have to deal with certain basics. I am talking about things that will make you go through life comfortably in the short, medium and long-term, should the money you invest end up in a 'dingy black hole' – refuse to return. These basics are home and mortgage, emergency funds, pension, life insurance and your dependants.

Once they are in place, the ground is prepared for further saving or investment.

The next step is to clarify and specify your objectives for investment. You should decide whether, for example, you want to save to provide for income now or for future growth. Perhaps you opt to invest towards income during retirement or towards higher education for your children. Your objectives have to suit your personal circumstances – e.g. health, family, and how long you want to invest. It is also necessary to understand your attitude towards risk and know just how much risk you are prepared to take. Having identified your objective and ascertained your risk tolerance, you can then put an investment strategy in place.

Research in 1999 uncovered about 30,000 financial products on the market, a figure which is bound to increase with the passage of time. The number of products that exist is not as important as the quality of choice the investor will make. In choosing a financial product, you should make the most of your hard-earned money. You should try to get a good deal, but not at the expense of grabbing a product that does not agree with your personal circumstances. Some seemingly cheap products don't always end up cheap in the end! Just make sure your money works hard enough for you. Avoid high charges as they eat into long-term returns and do keep your eyes open for hidden charges. Also be on the look out for withdrawal charges and the magnitudes of regular payments, and ensure they are satisfactory. Note that there are normally high penalty charges for early withdrawal especially in investment-based life insurance policies.

As aforementioned, risk forms part and parcel of investment and should not put off any investor. It should, however, be appropriately managed and contained as much as possible. It is essential to understand the risk attached to any product you choose and ensure it is within the comfort zone of the risk you can stomach.

With financial products chosen, and the strategy in progress, it is necessary to stand back from your investment, from time to time, and review it to establish how well the plan is functioning. Personal circumstances change at different stages in one's life, and call for related alterations in the investor's objectives, and hence investment strategy. Regular reviews will increase the chances of identifying malfunctioning securities and making timely and necessary adjustments. It will be rewarding to keep your eyes wide open on current market rates and move your instant savings around to earn as much return as possible.

Every investor should protect himself as much as possible through all the stages in the investment process discussed above, in order to ensure success. It is true that that financial services in the UK have been very much reformed in recent times and that the Consumers' Association and the Financial Services Authority are doing the best they can to ward off scandals. The onus is, nonetheless, on the investor to be on his guard against fraudsters and unscrupulous investment companies. The way to protect oneself is not to be blindfold before taking a plunge, and always remembering this: "if it is too good to be true, then it probably is!"

Which Way Will The Market Move?

Some fund managers attempt to predict the movement of the stock market in order to organize their portfolios in a way that will produce higher returns. It has as well been suggested by some investment experts that investors time the market to see whether it is going to rise or fall before taking a plunge. But let's face it; is it possible to tell whether the market is going to move up or down?

About thirty years ago, in spite of fluctuations in the stock market, it proved to deliver high returns in the long-run. A lot has happened, however, since the fatalities of 11 September 2001. Prices went downhill on the stock market. The situation was worsened by the scandals of Enron and WorldCom, which span late 2001 to early 2002. Investors lost their faith in the earnings and profits that were published in the accounts of US companies. This knocked off the confidence investors had in the US stock markets, and share prices saw a further depression. The effect was not contained in the US but trickled down to other stock markets, leading to a general fall in share prices world-wide.

Subsequent occurrences such as the prolonged and on-going war in Iraq, as well as various terrorist bomb attempts in the UK and other European countries have made the stock market even more turbulent. The cumulative impact of all these occurrences has been the creation of stock markets shrouded in a shadow of investment uncertainty.

Recent research has caused realism to hit investors really hard. It is time to accept the fact that the high returns that used to be enjoyed by investors about thirty years ago is non-existent now, and will not be produced in the future. Although an investment in shares over a long-term can still produce returns superior to safer asset classes, the returns attained will not be as high as they used to be. Let me be brutally frank with every investor; the good old days are gone and never to come back. Year 2002 saw a price fall of nearly 43 % from historic highs, and there hasn't being much improvement since.

Stock market returns have being revised downwards. One reason is that the UK is presently experiencing an era of low levels of inflation and financial regulators see it fit and realistic to keep expected returns low. The second reason is that the stock market saw high returns for twenty years or so before 11 September, and there are doubts that the same momentum will be maintained.

An investment in shares has historically proven to provide higher returns than safer securities like gilts, bonds and bank deposits. Until recently, experts used to hold the notion that an investment in shares had to be sustained for at least five years, in order to obtain superior profits. Times have changed, and the reality is now kicking in; experts are now of the opinion that an investment in shares has to be held for a minimum of ten years to provide the same superior returns that were experienced in the past.

The truth is that it is not possible to predict how the market will behave; the dot-com bubble burst is a case in point. The reality that the stock market will produce lower returns than it used to should be embraced and internalised by investors. Most people will not make a fortune on the market overnight. An investment in the stock market with a long-term view in mind, as well as controlling and minimising the risk involved is the best approach.

The Basics to Consider Before Investing

Cast your mind back to your childhood days, and recall the sandcastle you built at the beach on that bright summer's day. If you remember clearly, the best castle that you managed to erect was the one you went to great lengths to build a very good base for. It is the same with investment strategies; a very successful one has to stand on some basic blocks which are: home, pension, dependants and emergency fund.

Are you renting or buying your home? If you are buying your home, you are perhaps undertaking the largest investment commitment in your entire lifetime. It is important to make sure that the size and the terms of the mortgage suit your personal circumstances. Mortgage interest rates are usually higher than the rate you can earn on a bank, building society or other interest bearing security. Thus if you have funds to invest, it might be sensible to reduce the mortgage amount by a lump sum payment. The decision should be based on a thorough research and a comparison of various interest rates with that of the mortgage interest rate.

You should also make sufficient provision for your retirement. State pension is going to be very little in the future, and many employers are no longer offering final salary schemes to employees. Contribution rates are also being cut by employers. You should find out what your state pension, occupational pension and savings will amount to during retirement and if not sufficient, make provision for extra savings. If you are self-employed, you should consider a personal pension or stakeholder pension scheme.

Family concerns form a big part of the basics to look at before investing. How would your spouse or children survive if you should die tomorrow? Does your spouse have to return to work a lot earlier than planned? Will there be enough money to pay for childcare, if your spouse has to start working immediately? A common way of providing for these eventualities is through a life insurance policy. Term insurance is the cheapest kind that can be considered.

It is also necessary to have some money sitting intact and safely in an account to deal with emergencies. It should be possible to access this money instantly or on very short notice. This is the 'emergency' fund, and it will be a bad practice to put it in a unit trust or share, which can lead to fluctuations in the value of the underlying amount. An instant-access ISA will be a wise choice of home for such a fund. At the most, the notice period should be a week.

Dealing with other investments before considering the basics is like placing the cart before the horse. The basics, without exception, should be always dealt with before attempting to invest any funds. It is advisable to separate the basics from the other investments in a strategy. This will rid the plan of confusion and provide peace of mind for the investor. At regular periods when there are major adjustments to be done in the plan, it is again necessary to ensure that all the basics have been revised and dealt with first.

Merits and Demerits of Tracker (Index) Funds

Actively managed funds such as unit trusts, investment trusts and OEIC, were in existence before the advent of tracker or index funds. The latter sprung up because actively managed funds on average, failed to outperform the market index. Index funds have several advantages, but not without a downside.

What fund managers of actively managed funds try to do is to beat the market by predicting market movements and the movements of individual stocks relative to the market. Consistently succeeding in such forecast is, however, not possible if the efficient market hypothesis holds. Tracker funds, by composing a portfolio very similar to the stock index, have proved in the long-term, to provide returns that match those of the market, and higher than the returns of actively managed funds.

One advantage tracker funds have over actively managed funds is the lack of management risk. The performances of fund managers vary immensely. Some in the short term manage to outperform the stock index whilst others underperform. Research shows that whether a fund outperforms or underperforms the market index depends merely on chance. In other words, it is not possible to say which direction the performance of a fund will take, and this leads to what is known as 'management risk'. This type of risk is non-existent in an index fund, since the manager has to only attempt to mirror the construct and performance of the stock market.

A more important merit of tracker funds is the cheaper means of investments they provide for investors. On average, an investor has to incur an initial charge of about 6 % of the amount invested in a unit trust in the UK. There will as well be an annual charge for fund management of about 1.5 %, and then transaction costs also attracting something in the region of 1 % per year. These figures are quite high compared to those of tracker funds which have no initial charge, have minimal transaction costs and only 0.5 % of the amount invested charged annually for management.

Tracker funds by their very nature have very well diversified portfolios which result in the spreading of risk. Actively managed funds are normally not sufficiently diversified, as the main goal is one of performance and not of reducing risk. They can be tilted towards a particular sector or industry that the fund managers believe can help achieve their high return objective.

A drawback of index funds is the practice of excluding shares of small companies from their portfolios. For example, the FT All Share in the UK contains the shares of only 800 companies, and excludes those of about 1000 companies, on grounds of having a small capitalisation. Actively managed funds, however, do not distinguish between small companies and large ones, as long as their selection can lead to a return advantage over the stock index.

The exclusion of some shares from the portfolios of index funds can lead to weaknesses in mirroring the stock index, since the resulting portfolios will not be representative of the market as a whole. This can lead to returns lower than that of the stock market, and the disparity in return is known as the tracking error. The greater the number of shares included in the portfolio of the tracker fund, the more improved the replication of the stock index will be, but with an associated rise in transaction cost.

The shares of stock indices change. New ones move in and some old ones move out. These changes will necessitate alterations in the shares of tracker funds as well, and tracking errors can result from the time that has to lapse before appropriate share changes are implemented. If there are a lot of tracker funds, shares that are leaving the stock index will be sold cheaply, and those that are entering will be bought at high prices. This price trend in the buying and selling of shares does negatively impact on the returns of tracker funds.

Opinions of experts are quite divided as regards which is superior – actively managed funds or tracker funds. Nevertheless, research by the Financial Services Authority (FSA), shows that a good fund performance in the past does not guarantee a good performance in the future, although a bad performance normally signals a bad one in the future. It will as such be a real chore to attempt to distinguish between a good actively managed fund and a bad one. The choice should be based on a lot of fact finding. Whenever in doubt, an investment in a tracker fund should suffice.

Some Short Term Maturity Instruments

It is necessary and quite rewarding to match the time horizon of one's needs with the right type of savings. When considering saving for returns to satisfy short-term needs, bank and building society deposits are what usually come to mind. There are albeit several other short-maturity instruments in the money market that can pique your interest in short-term savings. These are: certificates of deposits (CDs), bills and commercial papers.

Certificates of deposits constitute a variant of deposits. They provide benefits for both the holder and the issuer alike. It is a wholesale instrument, and hence employed by companies but out of the reach of retail investors, except indirectly through institutional investors. It entails a company depositing money with a bank (the issuer) for a specific period of time (usually three months), in exchange for a certificate or document that states what the maturity date is and how much total amount (deposit plus interest) will be paid when the deposit matures. One good feature of CDs is that they can be sold in the money market and are hence more liquid to the holder than an ordinary time deposit. To the holder, it provides more liquidity, and accordingly attracts less interest from the bank. Thus with a CD, the holder can encash the certificate before maturity, and the bank can borrow at an interest rate less than it would have borrowed if it was taking an ordinary deposit.

Bills form a means of short-term borrowing for companies and the government. When issued by the government they are known as Treasury Bills and normally have a maturity of three or six months. Treasury bills do not pay interest but attract capital gains. What happens is that the government sells the bills through auction (tender). There are two kinds of auctions used: bid price auction and striking price auction. In a bid price auction, the buyer pays the price that is bid whilst the same price is paid by buyers in a striking price auction. In both cases, however, the bills are sold at the highest price. Capital gain results because the bills are sold at prices lower than their redemption price.

There is another type of bill, known as exchange bill that is used to enhance trading. An owner of goods draws a bill for the goods delivered, and the buyer signs the bill, confirming that payment of a specific amount will be made on a certain date (up to twelve months from date of issue). To reduce the risk of default, some bills are guaranteed by banks, when they become known as bank bills. The advantage of using bills is that they are negotiable. The holder can sell it at a discount to receive cash sooner than the maturity date, in order to be able to continue more efficiently with business operations. To the buyer, it provides the benefit of being able to defer payment till the maturity date.

Commercial paper is a wholesale instrument that is issued by companies as a means of borrowing. Like CDs, the private investor has no access to it, except through institutional investors such as unit trusts, or via money market funds. A company normally plans a borrowing programme of taking a loan of, say, £50 million over a period of four years. The issue is carried out by a bank or a series of banks, who will place the commercial papers with prospective investors.

The papers are not all issued at once, but are spaced out accordingly as need for the money arises. Thus within the four year programme, there will be a cocktail of redemption of loans plus interests that have matured and issues of new commercial papers. Note that with all the borrowings the issue is carried out by a bank or a series of banks and will fall within the confines of a total of £50 million.

As business environments are becoming increasingly hypercompetitive, a good knowledge of the benefits provided by some of these short-maturity instruments can make the difference between an enterprise that goes bust and the one that survives and perhaps gains a competitive edge. It's all a matter of being able to match one's needs with the appropriate saving or borrowing instrument.

Are Deposits Really Risk Free?

Normally when people hear 'risky investments' their attention is immediately switched to stock market securities such as bonds and especially shares. Bank and building society deposits never come to mind, because they are considered very safe. This attitude towards deposits manifests because only one type of risk called capital risk is being considered. Inflation and income risks which equally affect deposits are overlooked. An exposition of inflation and income risks will show that bank and building society deposits are not as risk-free as they are thought to be.

Capital risk is the probability that the price or value of an asset will fall due to market fluctuations. The notion held by many people about deposits is right when only capital risk is considered. This is because uncertainty in the money market does not affect the value of bank and building society deposits per se; it is the interest rate that suffers. Conversely stock market securities such bonds and shares are very susceptible to changes in value due to fluctuations in the market.

Inflation risk is the probability of an asset losing its purchasing power. It does rob money of its ability to buy the same 'basket' of goods as it could previously do. Let's say you deposit your money in the bank or building society in year one, intent on withdrawing it plus accumulated interest in year three, to buy a car at a specific price. Take it inflation then was 2.5 %. At the time of withdrawal, if inflation shoots up to 5 %, you will receive your principal and the amassed interest as promised by the bank, but you cannot buy the car as envisaged, because the price of the car would have shot up, all things being equal, thanks to inflation. Inflation erodes the purchasing power of deposits and their interests, even when compounded. In other words, deposits are prone to inflation risk.

Indeed, shares in the long-term have provided returns that are proportionately higher than inflation rates, and hence can stomach inflation better than bank and building society deposits.

Income risk is the probability that interest or dividends will fall. Bank and building society interest rates depend on the economy's short-term interest rate. Some people's main reason for investing in deposits or stock market securities is to receive regular income payments. When the economy's short-term interest rate falls, bank and building society interest rates tend to fall as well, and can be a blow to income-seeking investors. Deposits are thus subject to income risk, and so are bonds. Annuities are also exposed to income risk, due to variations in long-term interest rates. There is uncertainty regarding how much dividends are paid by a company; it is the directors who decide, and sometimes for growth purposes, can decide to pay nothing. Shares, in spite of this uncertainty, have proven to provide much higher returns than deposits and bonds alike in the long-term. In the long-run, the good times offset the bad ones; they can withstand income risk a lot better.

The hard truth is that bank and building society deposits are not as risk-free as they are usually thought to be. They are prone to inflation and income risks just like bonds and shares. To add to the surprise, although investments in shares have high capital risk, they are relatively safer in terms of inflation and income risks.

The Biases Investors Suffer From

I personally feel a host of people lose money in their investment not because of the capricious nature of the stock market but because of biases in the important investment decisions they make. Many investors unwittingly suffer from one form of bias or the other. In this discussion, I will draw the reader's attention to the various forms of biases that investors suffer from. The biases investors primarily suffer from are: overconfidence, representativeness, conservatism, narrow framing and ambiguity aversion.

Self-attribution bias contributes to overconfidence bias. In self-attribution bias the investor is very quick to attribute the good results of investment decisions to himself and blame others or come up with excuses when things don't work according to plan. This leads to overconfidence in one's ability to select the right shares for a portfolio. It also leads to an irrational behaviour of not sufficiently diversifying one's portfolio to reduce risk. Overconfidence bias supports the over-reaction hypothesis which states that markets rise too high when they rise and fall too low when they fall. When an overconfident person thinks the market will rise he invests enthusiastically, hence causing the market to rise more than necessary. On the other hand, a feeling that the market will fall leads to a progressively decreasing investment which causes the market to fall more than necessary. Overconfidence also explains why some investors trade more often, although they have to pay high charges every time they buy or sell shares.

Representativeness is to do with one projecting past successes or failures as also happening in the future. Thus some investors will invest a lot in a particular share just because it performed well in the past, or invest less in a security because it underperformed in the past. This sort of action or decision takes place in spite of concrete evidence that future performances cannot be guaranteed by past performances on the stock market. It is a form of bias.

Conservatism refers to a slow response to information or events. Research shows that a lot of investors only buy shares when it is about to peak in price and sell when it is just about to trough.

Narrow framing has to do with considering things from a smaller perspective than it should be. Looking at a long-term investment from a short-term perspective is a good example. Some investors anxiously monitor daily changes in the prices of securities in a portfolio targeted at achieving an objective in forty years' time. Others as a result of this bias consider the volatility of the constituent securities of their portfolios, instead of looking at the risk of the portfolio as a whole. This can result in a rather meagre investment, since individual securities in a portfolio tend to be more volatile than the portfolio itself.

Bias of ambiguity concerns investors' preparedness to invest only in companies they know more about. A lot of investors prefer investing in companies in their own countries, even if investment in other countries can provide higher returns and also help to reduce risk.

One bias that is very closely related to narrow framing is that of retrievability, in which investors pay more attention to information that they can readily recall. Some investors will only support statements that coincide with their views, rejecting those that oppose the notion they hold. Others suffer from illusion of control. Some investors feel they are really in control of the investment situation, when in actual fact they are not. This type of bias explains why many investors pursue actively managed funds, irrespective of research findings that tracker funds outperform actively managed ones in the long-term.

Great dividends can be expected if the investor will use the above-mentioned biases as a checklist when making important investment decisions. Biases can warp the decision making mind of an investor, and foster irrationality and lack of objectivity. Taking appropriate measures to eschew biases is the first step towards investment success.

Implications of Rising Powers of Institutional Investors

Institutional investors have always enjoyed some advantages over the private investor. In fact in recent times, they are growing relentlessly powerful. This increase in power has a lot of implications, most of which are social and corporate.

In 1957, research showed that there was a ratio of one institutional investor to five private investors investing directly in the stock market. This figure rose to a dramatic three to four in year 2003. Further increase in strength can be expected in connection with pension savings. The jump in the proportion of retirees to those who are in work coupled with the rise in life expectancy has resulted in what is now commonly known as the 'demographic time bomb'. One way around this pension problem is to increase the amount of pension savings by those still working, in order to avoid poverty during retirement. This is bound to augment the powers of institutional investors which are already escalating.

This increase in the power of institutional investors will make the private investor who decides to go solo more disadvantaged than it has ever been. The private investor already has less technical expertise than the fund manager who runs, say, a unit trust. He does not have access to the scale of economies enjoyed by institutions, in terms of cuts in 'bulk' transaction costs and commissions, research and so on. The complicated analytical gadgets that are taken for granted by the fund manager are totally out of the reach of the private investor. What then will be the fate of the small investor if institutional investors are going to grow even stronger than they are now? In the first place the retail investor will be toiling in vain to identify winners in companies, especially in the blue chips, as he has to rely on only superficial media information.

There will also be social implications of the imminent rise in power of institutional investors. The distinction between owner and work will be extinct in due course. This can be much better understood, when one thinks in 'aggregate' terms. You see workers invest indirectly through life insurance policies, pension schemes and so on, and these institutional investors go on further to invest the pooled funds in a wide variety of companies. In other words if we consider the investments in all companies which represents 'owner' as one collective investment like a big cake, and a worker is given a knife, he/she can identify and cut a portion of the big cake (the owner) as the part that belongs to him or her. With the piece of the cake that is cut in hand, symbolically speaking, we have a worker being an owner as well.

There will also be implications on corporate governance. Corporate governance involves the control of companies. Until recently 'managerial capitalism' was the order of the day. Managers ignored their main objective of adding value to shareholders, and concentrated on the satisfaction of their own self-interest. This led to what is commonly called lack of 'goal congruence'. Managers could get away with this sort of practice, because shareholders were mainly fragmented and had no power. The increase in the number and powers of institutional investors has led to fewer and more concentrated shareholders with potent voting rights. These shareholders can vote directors out of their positions, should they digress from adding value to the shareholder. It is hoped that one impact of this hike in power will be to lead to goal congruence in firms.

It is quite a daunting task to attempt to come up with anything that might impede the advancement of institutional investors. Their rise in power has got the full backing of the 'Almighty' pension problem, and what is going to stop it? "If you can't beat the man, join him"; perhaps the small investor who has been going solo can bring all the hassle to a close, by jumping on the accelerating wagon of institutional investors.

How to Value Shares

The equity market is fairly capricious and can lead to losses. With care and due judgment in valuing shares, however, substantial profits can be made over and above what can be achieved with relatively less risky securities such as bonds, gilts and bank deposits. 'Dividend yield', 'price earnings (P/E) ratio' and 'net asset value' are the three main tools used in valuing stocks (shares).

Dividend yield gives an indication of the investor's return for holding the share. It is obtained by dividing dividend per share by the current market price of the share. Dividend per share is the total dividend paid in the most recent twelve months divided by the total outstanding shares. Dividend yield is expressed as a percentage. Let's assume, for example, the dividends paid by company 'A' in the most recent twelve months total £4 million and there are 4 million shares outstanding. Let's say the current market price of the company is £20. The dividend per share is £4million/4 million, which is £1 per share. The dividend yield will thus be given by (£1 divided by £20) times 100, which is 5 %. This figure 5 % means that the investor can expect to earn a return of 5p for every pound he invests in the share.

Traditionally, investors prefer companies with high dividend yields to those with lower ones. A high dividend yield implies that the share is under-priced, and that future dividends will not be higher than previous ones. A low dividend yield, on the contrary, means the share is over-priced and future dividends might be higher.

P/E ratio is a very important ratio for valuing the performance of a share. It is arrived at by dividing the current market price by the earnings per share. For example, if the current market price of a company is £30 and the earnings per share is £5 per share, then the P/E ratio is £30 divided by £5 which is 6. Note that no percentage or unit is attached to the figure. P/E ratio provides two lots of information, primarily. It does give the investor a rough idea of the pay-back period for the amount of money invested in each share. In the example above, for instance, a P/E ratio of 6 informs the investor that it will take 6 years of receiving returns of £5 per share per year, to recoup the £30 used in buying one share. Since there is a lot of variation in the dividends paid by companies over the years, it can be argued that P/E ratios do not provide very accurate pay-back information.

It does, however, provide a fairly accurate view of the growth potential of the share. It portrays the extent to which the market is optimistic about the stock, and its expectation of the share's future growth. A P/E ratio of 1 means the share is seen with a lot of pessimism, whereas a figure of 20 means the share is looked at favourably by investors. Recent research has, nevertheless, shown that shares with low P/E ratios outperform those with high ones. It is perhaps wise to take the middle road, and avoid shares with very low or extremely high P/E ratios.

The shares or units of organizations such as mutual funds and investment companies are valued using 'net asset value'. This is obtained by subtracting the total liabilities of the firm from its total assets. For instance, if the total assets of the mutual fund is £100 million, and its liabilities sum up to £10 million, then the net asset value is £100 million minus £10 million, which gives £90 million. The value of each unit or share is then arrived at by dividing the net asset value by the units or shares outstanding. In this example, if there are 2 million units outstanding, the 'per unit net asset value' is £90 million divided by 2 million which is £45 per unit. Net asset value as well as per share/unit net asset values are revised daily and published in newspapers.

None of these tools is perfect as a valuation device, but they are definitely superior to just carrying out judgement by speculating. When there is any doubt, moderation should be employed in the choice of the right P/E ratio, dividend yield, or net asset value. It is also advisable to find out the reasons behind the magnitudes of the figures you deal with.

Is the Media Useful to Investors?

Investors fall into two broad categories, namely: individual investors and institutional investors. If I was asked this question: Is the media useful to investors? My response will be a 'yes' for institutional investors, but as regards individual investors, I'd say, "Hold on a minute, while I think about it." Let's see why this kind of answer.

Investment news in the media is useful in the assessment of the performance of fund managers. Its benefit to the individual investor is, however, questionable. The problem is that many investors confuse media news with financial advice. They as such select the securities for their portfolios, based solely on information from the media, paying no heed whatsoever to a financial advisor. This practice results in frustration and substantial losses in the future.

When you have a mild headache, you can dash to the pharmacy to buy your own prescribed medication, take it, and most likely you will get better. On the other hand, if your ailment is grave, your instincts will tell you to consult a doctor (an expert) to carry out a diagnosis and to issue a prescription. Consulting the doctor can mean the difference between life and death. Similarly, it makes sense to solicit help from a financial advisor (an expert) when the investor has to deal with a complex combination of securities. An attempt to base the investment decision on information from the media can be devastating.

It is worth remembering that there is fierce competition in the media sector, and firms find it necessary to broadcast and publish hot news in order to survive and to gain a competitive edge. As a result, a lot of media news is packaged to look more attractive and usually blown out of proportion. Such news give rise to hot and sizzling securities that lure a host of investors only to dash their hopes in due course. Media information stirs up fear in investors during 'bears' (prices fall) and creates greed during 'bulls' (prices rise). A lot of investors have abandoned their financial plans and their financial advisors with the advent of 'hot' securities, to their own detriment.

Arguably, if the investor will research ardently and in-depth before constructing the portfolio, media news is of very little importance. We all know that investment is a long haul process. If securities are chosen properly and conscientiously, what is the use in disturbing one's investment, due to media news.

An investment is like a carrot. If you keep digging around it, to check its well-being, it will wilt. However, if it is left alone, it will flourish. It is like a cake of soap; the more it is touched, the smaller it becomes.

Whilst information from the media can be useful for the evaluation of performance of fund managers, it is dysfunctional to the individual investor. It is noise in his life and has to be reduced to the bare minimum, to encourage adherence to financial plans, and hence long-term achievement of financial goals. In this era when the investor is bombarded with investment news from every angle, it is advisable to keep some ear plugs to hand, to protect oneself from any negative influences and vibrations.

Who Is To Blame? Investor or Financial Advisor?

When financial plans fail to achieve the financial objectives aimed at, there is normally a lot of blame-laying. Indeed some advisors even get fired along the way. But let us be brutally honest with each other. Who is to blame? The investor or the financial advisor?

It is very difficult to answer this question due to the complexity of the financial planning process. I feel strongly that a general answer will be invalid, and that it is sensible to take each individual case in isolation, as a result of disparity in circumstances.

Let us have a close look at the question by considering the financial planning process in detail. Perhaps it will shed some light on who might go wayward in role play. It is usual for the financial planning process to start with a lot of questions pounded by the advisor to try to get to know his/her client. The idea is a step in the right direction, but can there be anything wrong with the process itself? I believe you got this answer right; it is a 'yes'. A number of things can go wrong during this 'interviewing' stage.

Done professionally, the financial advisor is to do only about 20 % of the talking and permit the client to use the remaining 80 % to hopefully, pour his heart out. The figures are based on what is known as the 'Pareto Rule' in sales; I wouldn't want to digress into that now, though. What I am saying, in effect, is that the advisor should listen attentively most of the time, and allow the client to do most of the talking. It is entirely the wrong time to be thinking about what types of services or products will be suitable for the investor. Rather, a close attention should be paid to the subtext as well as the body language of the investor, and endeavour to take note of any salient clues. It must be remembered that only about 7 % of communication occurs in speech! Success at this stage also depends very much on the range of questions that are asked and how relevant they are.

The investor has a major part to play here. He/she must embrace the fact that financial planning is a two-way process and does fail when the effort gets one-sided. The respective roles are not any different from those of a doctor and a patient, with the investor taking the latter role. The investor is supposed to be as open and frank as possible when answering questions. If done properly, some of the questions will come off as prying into one's private life, but the hard truth is that they must be correctly and joyously answered, if one is striving for success in investment. Remember the doctor can only be chanced to issue a sterling prescription, with the full support of the patient during the 'diagnosis' stage. The advisor cannot work the magic if he does not get to know his client very well.

A lot of issues, including age, risk tolerance, family matters, purpose for money, financial objectives, income, amounts owed, existing assets, life expectancy, retirement age, and so on have to be touched on in the 'interview'. The element that takes most time and skill to ascertain is the 'risk tolerance level'. It is also normally quite difficult for investors to tell the difference between 'purposes' for their money, and their financial goals.

The 'purpose' for money is the broad context into which the goals fit. An example might help to clarify this. Somebody might have a purpose of achieving a very comfortable retirement period. Into this general idea one can have financial objectives (normally quantified) of having say access to £5 million to provide an income of say £50,000 a year, to help maintain the lifestyle he/she is living now.

All things being equal, a financial plan is drawn, and then put into action. At this stage both parties have a role to play. It is important that the investor trusts and maintains enough faith in the advisor and the plan, so as to stick to the latter, irrespective of fluctuations in stock market. The role of the advisor here will be to stay as close as possible throughout the period of implementation, carrying out relevant reviews and adjustments in the plan when changes in the stock market warrant. It is also beneficial if the advisor is there to calm the fears of the client especially during 'bears' (when prices fall) and avoid greed, on the part of the investor during 'bulls' (when prices rise). This will be a step in the right direction to encourage the client to stick to the financial plan, and hence assuming it is a powerful one, raise the likelihood of achieving the financial objectives.

I hope you have decided by now that it is perhaps not easy or right to point fingers when a financial plan does not achieve its purpose. There are so many factors to consider, and at each stage in the process of planning and execution, either parties can excel or underperform. My advice is: keep your hands in your pockets, and you will be saved the trouble of pointing your finger at the wrong person.

Unit Trust Versus Investment Trust

Considering the high dealing cost in share transactions, for the private investor, it is not worth the trouble investing less than £2000 in shares. In fact one will chuck himself into a gambling or speculation situation unless he/she is prepared to part with a whooping £50,000 investment in shares. One way around this is to invest in unit trusts or investment trusts, both of which pool funds of private investors together and invest in a wide variety of shares, corporate bonds, gilts, properties and other securities, locally and internationally. Many investors, however, find it difficult to tell the two kinds of trusts apart, as they are similar in many respects. There are remarkable differences between unit trusts and investment trusts and it is worth considering them.

The main problem area is in understanding the unusual configuration of a unit trust. Let's assume there are 1000 private investors, each with £5000 to invest. These funds can then be pooled together to give a total of £5 million. The fund managers then proceed to invest this £5 million in shares, and other securities. Assume the value of the investment remains fixed, and the fund managers decide to start with 1 million units. Then each unit is worth £5 million divided by 1 million, which gives each unit a value of £5. Remember that the investors contributed equally (£5000), and if there are 1000 of them then each is entitled to 1000 units out of the total of 1 million units. To check the arithmetic, multiply the 1000 units of each contributor by the value of each unit (£5) and you arrive at the £5000, which is the amount each investor contributed. I hope you see how it works. Hence assuming the underlying securities into which the fund managers invested doubles in value, so that the total investment of the fund is worth £10 million, then the price of each unit becomes £10 (obtained from £10 million divided by the 1 million units). The value of each contributor's investment then rises to £10 times 1000 units (the original entitlement) to give £10,000 (value doubled, just like the underlying securities). It can thus be said that the price of a unit depends on the value of the underlying securities of the fund at any point in time.

Investment trusts, unlike unit trusts are floated companies with shareholders. In fact it is structured very much like other public companies, except that instead of producing goods or providing services, it is limited to investing in shares, bonds, gilts, other securities and in properties. Its investments are spelt out in the Memorandum, Articles and Prospectus of the company, whereas the operations and investments of a unit trust are outlined in the 'trust deed'. As regards pricing, unlike unit trusts, the price of an investment trust's share is decided by the forces of demand and supply in the market. One disadvantage in putting one's money in investment trust, which is lacking in a unit trust, is the discount to net asset value it is normally susceptible to. This discount is supposed to make the shares of the trust competitive relative to its underlying securities.

Apart from money paid towards the unit itself, there are fixed charges of about 5 % of the total amount invested in a unit trust, plus an annual fee of between 1 and 1.5 %. The bid-offer spread, which goes to fund managers, is about 6 % for unit trusts. The cost of commission and other charges in investment trusts is much less than in unit trusts, except when one is investing a very small amount. The bid-offer spread in investment trusts becomes increasingly smaller with rising popularity, and hence liquidity of the trust's shares. It can vary from less than 1 % for a very popular trust to about 10 % for an unknown one.

The lower charges gives investment trusts a higher chance to grow, since the bulk of the investors' money goes into buying the actual securities.

Transactions within both unit and investment trusts are free of capital gain tax (CGT). Holders of units or shares in these trusts are also free of CGT up to a certain limit when they sell their holdings. Both unit trust and investment trust distribute income in the form of dividends and interests they receive from their diverse investments. Unit trusts allows such income to be reinvested, whilst some investment trusts don't permit reinvestment of income, or in some cases, only allows it to be put into an ISA.

Unit trusts are said to be 'open-ended' because they can increase the number of units in the fund, by taking money from a new member and buying more shares or other securities, or reduce the number of units when an investor wants to sell its units by selling out some of the underlying securities. Investment trusts are, nevertheless, limited in the size of their portfolio. Once issued, there is only a change of ownership of the same securities through buying and selling on the stock market. They can only increase the size of their portfolio through rights issue or scrip issue. Investment trusts are hence said to be 'closed ended'. The configuration of investment trusts rids them of the pressure that unit trusts suffer to sometimes part with some of their best securities just to satisfy an investor who wants to sell his units. Investment trusts, conversely, can part with their shares or other securities more strategically. It must be noted that both unit and investment trusts cut down paper work and administrative costs for the private investor, whilst spreading risk through the diverse investments.

As perhaps gathered from the discourse above, investment trusts and unit trusts have some common features, but both have advantages and disadvantages where they differ. It is entirely up to the investor to properly assess his needs and decide which of the two to go for. It wouldn't hurt investing in both, if you have the funds, as there are certain unit trusts that invest in investment trusts anyway.

Which Interest Rate?

Interest rates are the income on bank and building society deposits, and take different forms and sizes. It is essential that the investor develops an awareness of the types there are and how they differ from each other. As will soon be revealed, lack of such knowledge can lead to flawed decision making, with resultant investment losses.

The interest rate paid by banks and building societies can be fixed or variable, and depends on the economy's basic rate. Between the extremes of fixed and variable interest rates is the 'roll-over' type. An example is a six-month roll-over interest rate, in which the interest rate remains fixed for six months, and then changes to match the new current interest rate in the market.

Interest rates are normally paid semi-annually or annually. Compounding of interest rates comes into play when interest has to be paid more than once a year. The effective interest rate, which is also called the annual percentage rate (APR) is in this case greater than the stated annual rate. For example, if £100 is invested at an annual rate of 6 %, the money accumulated at the end of the year will be £106. If the interest is paid semi-annually, the APR is calculated as follows: the interest rate for both the 'first and second' six months will be half of 6 % which is 3 %. The money accumulated at the end of the year will as such be given by £100 times 1.03 times 1.03, giving £106.09. There is an increase of £6.09 which is equivalent to 6.09 % return on the £100 invested. Note that the APR is greater than the annual interest rate of 6 %.

Ability to distinguish between nominal and real interest rate is of utmost importance to the investor, if unnecessary losses have to be eluded. Nominal or market interest rate, is the conventionally stated interest rate, and does not make allowance for inflation. Inflation robs both the principal invested and the return of their purchasing powers, and has to be considered when making investment decisions. The 'real' interest rate allows for inflation. There is a relationship between 'real', 'nominal' and 'inflation' rates which will be a useful tool to the investor. Real interest rate is calculated by subtracting 1 from (nominal interest + 1) divided by (inflation rate + 1). Thus if £100 is invested at a 'nominal' rate of 3 % and inflation rate is 3 %, then the investor doesn't have to be celebrating, since the 'real' rate of return will be zero: [(1.03)/(1.03)] minus 1, which is zero. It is a good idea to also consider the effect of taxation on the 'real' interest rate.

Finally let us consider what is known as the redemption yield. Investment in bank and building society deposits provides only interest or interest yield as a return, whereas an investment in a bond provides a capital gain or loss in addition to the promised coupon. There is capital gain or loss because bonds are traded on the stock market and can lose or gain value due to market fluctuations. If a bond is purchased for £97 to be redeemed at £100. Let's say there is a coupon of £4 to be paid semi-annually. Thus at the end of the year there will be a total coupon of £8 paid on £97 invested, which amounts to 8.25 % p.a. [(8/97) x 100)] interest yield. If the bond is redeemed at £100, the gain in value of £3 amounts to 3.09 % p.a. [(3/97) x 100] capital gain. The total return or redemption yield is the sum of the interest yield and the capital gain which is 8.25 % plus 3.09 %, giving 11.34 % p.a.

The underlying purpose of any investment is to make returns to compensate the investor for the risk taken. There will always be a lot of options to choose from, and a thorough understanding of the varieties of interest being dealt with, can lead to a well-informed investment decision. This will go a long way to foster the maximization of 'real' expected returns, before and after tax.

How to Select Shares for Your Portfolio

Investors employ a multiplicity of techniques in choosing shares. What is common amongst the various methods is that they don't always work. The suggestions made in this discussion combined with common sense and good judgment should help to hone your stock selection skills.

The first step in the selection process is asking yourself a few questions to help clarify exactly what you want and expect from your investment. It is immensely necessary to endeavour to find out the amount of risk you are prepared to take. Look back and recall how you felt when you incurred some financial losses. Such memories, with some amount of honesty should help you to find out your level of risk tolerance.

Companies on the stock market are grouped on two main bases: in terms of similarity in size, and on grounds of carrying out the same activities (sector grouping). If your analysis shows you are risk-loving, then your focus should be on smaller companies or growth companies which are generally riskier, with potential for higher returns. If you happen to be the risk averse type or you want a share with minimum maintenance, then you want to consider large organisations, which have a lower tendency to go bust and can also serve as more reliable source of income. Such firms are known as 'blue chips'. Target shares in industries or sectors that will be positively impacted on by political ventures and economic trends.

After considering the category of companies you want to deal with, you should begin inspecting the dividend yields and P/E ratios of the companies. It is a good idea to be on the look out for companies with reasonably high dividend yields. A P/E ratio between 7 and 10 is very much recommended. Remember that a P/E ratio is only useful when compared to others. Consider companies with P/E ratios that are lower than those of competitors in the same industry, and also lower than the previous years' figures. The yearly sales and earning per share figures should ideally be increasing over the previous years. It's a good idea to consider growth companies that have fallen on hard times, but show signs of future recovery.

You should also decide how long you will be holding the share for. You will thus be on the alert, when it is time to get rid of the share. Higher returns will be earned when a share is held for a minimum of five years, with substantial savings in dealing expenses. This, nonetheless, does not mean that duds should not be turfed out before their planned disposal dates. Accordingly, a winner should not be gotten rid of just because it has had a decent run. Tact should be exercised before selling shares and it is a good technique to keep an eye on the next share to grab, once the old one is gone.

Do not catch a falling knife. Although it is good practice to buy cheap shares, some shares suffer a free fall in price, and stay cheaper and cheaper with the passage of time. These should be avoided. Also eschew shares recommended by newspapers and tipsheets. The explanation for this is that market makers also read newspapers, and by the time you lay hands on the share, every advantage it has would have been already siphoned out by professional investors, especially, if you're considering a blue chip. If you want to try your luck in securing a winner you may have to rummage financial statements of companies that have capitalisation less that £100 million. Such companies do not attract professionals, hopefully you can beat the market here.

It is almost impossible to outperform the market extensively. What you want to avoid is losses. A long-term goal of tracking the market, or better still performing slightly better than it, is quite realistic and dignified. You should decide to what extent you want to get involved with the management of the share. If you want to be mildly involved, you will be better off investing in mutual funds or investment trusts rather than picking your own shares. Be prepared to buy investment management, when necessary.

Private vs. Professional Investors

Proponents of pooled funds argue that there is a great uncertainty on the stock market, and that it is dangerous for the private investor to play there, as they get prone to high losses and costs. Although there is a grain of truth in this, the argument for holding an investment in a unit trust or investment trust is just as good as that for holding equities. In the long-term, returns from holding equities have outstripped returns from safer investments such as corporate bonds, gilts and deposits. In spite of these gains, the fact still remains that professional investors have some advantages over private investors. The advantages enjoyed by professionals span three main areas, namely:

(i) information gap

(ii) economies of scale and

(iii) expertise, and these shall be considered in turn.

Professional investors, fund managers to be specific, have become increasingly powerful as the strength of institutional investors has grown over recent years. In the course of using their powers to instil goal congruence in corporate governance, professionals have had more access to insider information from companies than the private investor. Directors are quick to part with such information if a denial will cost them their prestigious jobs. It is claimed that when the private investor buys a share in a company, he has bought ownership, implying access to information to help him to vote sensibly when making corporate decisions, but this is not what happens on the field. This disparity in information makes the private investor toil to no avail to identify a winner, as any benefits inherent in such shares must have already being factored into the price by the time they are discovered.

Private investors have to make do with usually adulterated media information on investment, whereas the professionals have sophisticated analytical machines and tools readily at their disposal, on the back of the strength of their pooled funds. As if this is not enough, there is as well the expertise they can flaunt.

Professional investors also gain enormous advantages by exercising economies of scale. This occurs in various aspects of their operations, including R&D (research and development), administration and transaction costs. The availability of greater financial resources to the professionals enables them to employ the services of experts to research into detail the companies, products, and services they want to invest in. A lot of cost is saved, since one expert can consider several companies, products and services on the same project. This is a benefit the private investor cannot dream of. There are impressive cost savings when it comes to paying fees and commissions on transactions, since a lot of the securities will be considered in bulk.

In spite of the above-mentioned advantages, one area in which the private investor beats the professional is 'flexibility'. The private investor only has to invest in a stock that will provide the desired return and does not have to invest just to keep up with the market, like the professional. Fund managers also have to operate within the confines of the styles prescribed by their trusts, whereas the private investor can employ a 'free' style in investment. Indeed, to his own detriment, he can sell all the shares in his portfolio, go and bask in the warm sunshine of Spain, and come back to invest whenever he wants; such flexibility is totally out of the reach of the professional. As an aside, with the application of due care and technique it is possible to select a share that will provide long-term returns, but there is no method for choosing a good fund manager.

It is true that there are fluctuations in the stock market and can lead to losses for the private investor. Equally, there are a lot of fund managers who make losses and fail to achieve their targeted returns. Either side of the coin has its own ups and downs, private investor or professional investor. It is perhaps wise to combine the two in a portfolio, to even out the negatives with the positives.

The Guises of Risk

In a way risk is not a bad thing. Just like oxygen, it has a bright as well as a dark side. We humans need to breath in oxygen to stay alive; the same oxygen can aid the combustion of our precious possessions. A certain amount of risk is needed to fuel the investment vehicle to provide our expected return. What matters is the quantity of risk that suits the individual investor.

It is quite painstaking to determine the risk tolerance level of an investor. This is because the tolerance level of risk is normally masked, and even when it is uncovered, does not remain the same for any given investor. It varies from time to time as situations change. An investor who at one point is aggressive in style can become conservative all of a sudden, after the death, say, of a family member, who used to be relied on to pick up the pieces of an aggressive investment strategy.

Another problem is the difficulty some investment professionals and novices alike experience in defining 'risk tolerance level'. Perhaps in the parlance of the layman, 'risk tolerance level' is the level of risk that can allow an investor to go to bed without worrying about what might go wrong. It measures the amount of loss that one is prepared to take without losing sleep and health.

Risk is sometimes also seen in the light of 'lost opportunities' as opposed to 'loss in the amount invested'. For example, if for fear of over-concentration an investor parts with some shares, only to see the share price soar in a couple of days, this can be seen as risk by some investors.

There is as well the divide between investors who see risk in absolute terms and those who see it in relative terms. Some investors set a limit for the proportion of their invested money they are prepared to lose, through price falls. They thus will deem an investment a success as long as there is a gain on the amount invested or if total losses fall within the confines of the limit set. Whether there is a gain or loss does not trigger any reaction from the other group, until the result has been compared to the performance of the securities of friends, relatives, or the stock market as a whole. For example if an investor who measures risk in relative terms gains an increase of 10 % in the amount invested, and the stock market rises by 15 %, the investment will not be seen as a success, because the security or portfolio was outperformed by the stock market.

Certain investors claim they are aggressive when their every action says otherwise. A case in point is a person who invests in a low risk portfolio, intent on guarding his wealth to provide for an easy retirement. The irony is that this same person for instance may be a spendthrift to the extent that he/she cannot stay on top of the financial plan that can guarantee the sort of future envisaged. If you see what I mean, this person is actually not risk-averse!

A common blunder committed by investors who see themselves as aggressive or conservative, is to ensure each security in their portfolio reflects the risk category they belong to. I mean if the investor thinks he is aggressive then every security in his portfolio must be aggressive and vice versa. Aggressiveness or conservatism should be measured in terms of the whole portfolio and not in terms of the constituent securities. Similarly, a successful investment does mean that every security in the portfolio has to perform well. In fact this is not the case in practice, and when it occurs then the portfolio was most likely not sufficiently diversified.

Emotion is the Forerunner of Investment Doom

A lot of investments fail to achieve their desired ends because of shortcomings both on the parts of the financial advisor and the investor. Of all the errors, emotional attachment displayed or concealed by investors is the most damaging to investment success. A dramatic increase in the success rate of investments will be experienced, if advisors will pay ample attention to the emotions of their clients, prior to figuring out any investment plan.

Investors are fond of using their diverse personalities to hide their deep-seated feelings about money and the 'true' amount of risk they can take. If the financial advisor does not employ an appropriate tack to ask relevant and in-depth questions to uncover the investor's actual risk tolerance, the investment plan is bound to go pear-shaped.

A rack of emotional attachment cases occur in the day to day dealings of financial advisors with investors. A client may come across as a very aggressive investor, when in fact, the risk-loving robe is a one-off, worn just to prove a point to somebody in or outside the family with whom the investor at that juncture wants to compete. Another investor may be attached to a particular share, because he/she in the past managed to use the security as a tool for enrichment. The share is the investor's 'baby' and in spite of a glaring indication that focusing on the security is unsafe, he/she just cannot let go – it has been drummed into the psyche. Some investors develop a negative and a chronic attitude towards an asset class because they were burned in the past by an excessive risk they undertook, or in certain cases, because of bitter experiences of friends or relations, details of which may not be to hand.

Emotion is a hindrance, whose very roots have to be dug out, before a brilliant financial plan can materialize. It should be exposed and tempered to the bare minimum, if not eradicated completely. It blinds vision, and clouds the mind of the investor, and as such, functions as a formidable roadblock to realistic and objective analysis. It has a tendency of creating concentration in investment plans, and as you probably know, this weakness is strong enough to snuff out the life of any investment. Somebody may decide to leave several millions sitting in one security or industry that has no prospects whatsoever, or allow the bulk of his/her wealth to be buried in the value of a holiday home in a country where the bottom of the real estate market is sure to fall off. Why? All in the name of 'omnipresent' emotional attachment.

The panacea is 'intelligent' probing that fosters objective thinking in the mind of the investor. Whether or not this will be achieved hinges on the level of expertise, experience and professional demeanour of the financial advisor. It is only fair to add that total openness and commitment to answering questions in detail should constitute the investor's quota towards success.

Financial advisors should make it a point to look beyond the façade of their clients, and lead them to the realisation of their 'genuine' selves – their specific attitude and feeling towards money; the level of risk they can really stomach. Such a move will wring out emotion and pave the way for a more confident design of a powerful investment strategy.

Why You Need Both Equities and Bonds in Your Portfolio

Every investment involves some amount of risk taking, and as a rational investor, your aim should be to maximise your returns as much as possible, to obtain the best compensation for whatever level of risk you decide to take. When it comes to earning interest, your savings can either go to the bank or building society or to bonds and gilts. Bonds and bank/building society deposits compete for the funds of individuals, and thus usually have the same trend (rise or fall) in interest rates and yield. Concerning yields, the longer the maturity, the higher the expected compensation or yield. In order to comprehend the need for both equities and bonds in your portfolio, you must first fathom the relationship between interest rates, inflation, strength of currency and the well-being of an economy.

When one invests in a share/equity, what has fundamentally happened is that an ownership has been purchased in the company that is being considered. This means that one can make decisions and also share in the profits of the firm. Profits are distributed in the form of dividends, and it is the directors of the firm that decide how much dividend they want to pay out of profits. In fact, where all profits are reserved for growth, no dividends at all are paid sometimes, a practice very typical of small and new companies. It must also be noted that the money that is invested, unlike an investment in bonds, cannot be redeemed. One good benefit of equities, though, is that it protects investors from the sting of inflation. This is because firms tend to make more profits and their shares tend to pick up value, as inflation rises. This shelter from inflation is nevertheless denied bond investors, whose real yields, will be very much impinged upon by a rise in inflation.

It is rewarding to be aware of the inverse relationship that exists between the price of bonds and interest rates. When interest rates rise, the price of bonds fall and vice versa. This is because as mentioned earlier, bank and building society deposits, vie for the funds of individuals. When interest rates rise, bank and building society deposits become more competitive, and it is necessary for the price of bonds to fall to compensate for the lower yields being paid. Conversely if interest rates fall, the price of bonds will rise, so that investors pay for the higher yields they can earn.

A booming economy normally has businesses as well as individuals chasing a lot of money to invest in production and to spend on day to day activities. The forces of demand and supply kick in, and hence increase the price of borrowing, which is the interest rate. A boom also tends to trigger inflation and a fall in currency, which benefits equity holders, but affects bond holders negatively as afore-said – a rise in interest rates leads to a fall in price of bonds, and the increase in inflation devours the real value of the yield. The opposite of this combination of effects can be anticipated during a recession. Since the future is fairly uncertain, and one cannot accurately predict whether there will be a boom or recession, an investment that encompasses both equities and bonds stands to gain whether there is economic recession or boom.

The bottom line is that a mix of equities and bonds in a portfolio allows the investor to even the downs of one security with the ups of the other, whether there is a boom or recession. It is akin to the benefits enjoyed by a man I know who goes to Africa during the winter months because the weather there, at that time of the year, is really sunny and dry. When the rainy season starts in June/July, he will be nowhere to be found! Where do you think he will be? Back in England to have his share of the brightness of summer! In effect the access to England and Africa, like having a mix of bonds and equities, does not make him experience the torture of bad weather.

Common Errors in Investments

The wide variety of securities that exist today, make the modern investor prone to all sorts of temptations to meddle with 'bad' investment. It is as such very rewarding for investors and prospective investors alike, to be able to recognise the fine divide between a 'good' investment, with a high chance of success, and one that will fail. Let's proceed then to learn to identify the common errors in investments.

One characteristic of a 'bad' investment is the absence of a well-defined strategy. Even if there is a strategy, its potency is a monumental determinant of success. A strategy of investing in a few securities in one or a couple of industries is not powerful enough. Such a scheme should be rectified by investing in more diverse security types chosen from various industries. This tactic is to help spread risk in the investment, to increase the chance of obtaining the expected returns.

It is an appalling practice to attempt to time the market – sell lows and buy highs. What every investor has to bear in mind is that fads only lead to frustration in investments, and anyway, when a security becomes popular, it no longer bears any advantage, because any benefits would have been already factored into the price of the security. There is a tendency for prices of a security to rise, fall, rise and fall and so on, in the short and medium-term. If one sells a low to buy a high, a loss may be incurred as it is very likely that the high will be bought at a time when it has reached its peak in price and just on the brink of establishing a trough. In so far as one researches sufficiently to invest in the right combination of securities, it is wise for the investor to keep calm when short and medium term fluctuations occur, and hold onto the existing portfolio consistently.

The habit of frequent trading is dysfunctional because it leads to excessive and unnecessary commission and transaction costs, all of which can massively reduce expected returns. It can be contended that the rewards that may be possibly gained from following fads and timing of the market are by far outweighed by the risks involved. The focus of an investment should be on the long-term returns rather than on short and medium-term advantages. There is evidence to support the fact that an average portfolio when held to maturity provides much greater returns than frequent selling and buying of the constituent securities. Apart from commissions and transaction costs that are saved in a buy-and-hold strategy, there are tax benefits also to be gained, reason being less tax is paid on securities in a portfolio held to maturity, than are paid in frequent trading.

A weak investment strategy has a bias towards equities or bonds. In the long-term shares have proven to amass greater returns than bonds. However, it is good investment practice to have fair amounts of equities and bonds in one's portfolio. An explanation for this is that returns from equities and bonds are affected differently by economic changes, and holding both securities in a portfolio, does guarantee some benefits irrespective of the change.

It is inadvisable to expose investment to fads and insider tips. If something is too good to be true then it probably is. Although every investment will have a trace of imperfection, a lot of grave errors can be eluded if the investor, without fail, bears the 'big' picture in mind, and takes a calculated risk, in order to secure a handsome return in the long-term.

A Walk Through the Financial Markets

A host of people fail in investment because of a lack of understanding of the financial markets. Knowing how the markets work and the kind of instruments available is a prerequisite for triumph in investment, just as knowledge of an alphabet is needed for excellence in a language. The UK financial market can be split into two: the Money Market and the Stock Exchange Market.

The Money Market is dominated by the high street banks and building societies. It deals mainly in short-term loans (normally between three to six months). The banks and building societies serve as intermediaries to funnel aggregates of deposits from individuals (who have excess money to save) to companies who want to borrow extra funds to support their operations.

Conversely, the Stock Exchange Market has to do with securities that are negotiable – can be bought and sold before the redemption time. The Stock Exchange Market can be essentially divided into the Primary Market and the Secondary Market. The Primary Market has to do with new issues of shares, gilts and bonds, whereas the Secondary Market is involved in the buying and the selling of second-hand shares, gilts and bonds. In fact, a greater majority of the transactions that occur on the Stock Exchange Market relate to the Secondary Market. Arguably, the Secondary Market is the linchpin of the Primary Market. This is because the main reason why investors buy shares and bonds in the first place is because they can sell it on the Secondary Market, whenever they want to. It must, however, be noted that a sale of a gilt or bond prior to its redemption is most likely to result in some amount of loss due to possible changes in interest rates.

It is advisable for investors considering long-term savings (between twenty and thirty years) to put their money in shares through pension funds and insurance policies. Those interested in earning fixed interests on their investments can consider gilts, which are relatively safe instruments by which the government usually borrows to help pay off its deficits. There are short gilts, with a maturity up to five years; medium gilts with a maturity between five and fifteen years, and long gilts with a maturity of fifteen years and above. Undated gilts are those without a redemption date; the interest payment goes on non-stop, without a redemption of the principal invested. Index-linked gilts have their interest payments and redemption amounts based on the level of inflation.

Bonds are another class of interest earning instruments that are traded on the Stock Exchange Market. They are issued by companies in order to raise extra loans to top-up loans that their level of credibility could help raise from the money market – the banks and so on. They have redemption dates and pay interest greater than that paid on gilts, because investing in such bonds have a much higher default risk than investing in government gilts. In the worst case scenario, the government can print money to pay off principal and interest on the issued gilts.

Whether you find yourself dealing in the Money Market or the Stock Exchange Market, the rule of thumb is to exercise great caution and to shop around as much as possible. Stock prices change very fast and timing, as well as awareness is of great essence.

Nature Backs Diversification in Investment

I am very interested in Nature and love everything about it – its timeless beauty, unsurpassed wisdom and the priceless lessons it attempts to teach investors. All these amazing attributes are founded on the principle of 'diversification'. Nature comprises various elements – weather, plants, animals, us human beings, the rivers, the seas, landscapes and so on. A common feature of each constituent element is 'diversification'. For example, there are various seasons: summer, autumn, winter and spring. Human beings come in their varied colours, heights and sizes, plus a multiplicity of temperaments. Nature unceasingly wants investors to embrace one mantra – 'diversification'.

Why does all-wise Nature keep going on and on about its philosophy of 'diversification'? There must be something good in it for the investor, whatever deal the Great Teacher has got to offer! What really is the benefit? I will walk you through some concepts of investment in a moment to help throw some light on the matter.

A basic principle that underlies investment is that there is a trade-off between risk and returns. This means that if one takes a high amount of risk he/she can expect to enjoy a proportionately high return and vice versa. Risk measures the probability of obtaining the expected returns. There are primarily two types of risk namely systematic or market risk and unsystematic risk. Systematic risk is unavoidable and is common to all firms. It has to do with broad factors such as inflation, interest rate changes, political instability and so on.

Unsystematic risk on the other hand, is based on inefficiencies in a particular firm, such as poor management, high employee turnover, etc. This kind of risk, however, unlike market risk, can be avoided through ample diversification. The relationship between risk and return is normally explained by the Capital Asset Pricing Model (CAPM) which is a further development of Markowitz's Portfolio Theory (MPT). The word 'portfolio' is the term used in investment theory to designate a collection of chosen securities. According to CAPM, an investor is only rewarded for the systematic risks on its securities and not its unsystematic risk. The justification for this is that when an investment is sufficiently diversified – comprises a combination of anything between about fifteen to twenty securities, then all the unsystematic risk is more or less diversified away. In effect, all that there will be left to reward, is the systematic risk, over which the firm has no control. The essence of diversification is therefore to reduce risk, whilst still ensuring the attainment of the expected return.

In fact, diversification as a tool to cut down on risk does make sense. Firms in whose securities investments are made are affected differently by various changes in the economy. Some firms do really badly during economic decline, and perform well, when there is economic boom. Other firms, however, rather perform well when there are economic hardships, and underperform when things are good. There are also the 'all-rounders', that excel irrespective of what the economic situation is. Different industries suffer a similar fate. Even in the most successful organizations, things can turn really grim. Nature is the epitome of this. Consider the magnificence of the rose flower in its varied shades of colours; yet it is not without its thorns! It is a good idea to invest in assorted securities in dissimilar industries, so that losses in certain securities can be made up for by the gains in others. Variation in the types of securities dealt in is also crucial.

There isn't much to be gained from putting all of one's eggs in the same basket. Let's assume you own a considerable amount of some high-quality, sparkling diamonds, and lived alone in your own house in a deprived area, with high risk of theft. Would you hide all the diamonds in the same place? You can answer yes; but I wouldn't. I will hide them in different places to increase my chance of having some left for me, should my house get burgled. This is all diversification is about; to reduce risk, yet maintaining or enhancing returns.

Traits of a Bogus Financial Advisor

It has become a common occurrence for people, especially those in the middle and upper class brackets to solicit the services of financial advisors. Financial advisors, like any other professionals fall into two main categories: the true expert and the bogus. The begging question is: how does one tell the two apart? I personally think there is a fine line between the two categories and one will have to keep his eyes open, ears attuned and wits alert, in order to realize the difference.

Essentially, a financial advisor is supposed to ask his/her prospect necessary and sufficient questions to unveil his/her personal circumstances and 'actual' financial needs and objectives. It is important that the level of risk the prospect is comfortable with is ascertained during the 'diagnosis'. A 'qualification' of the prospect by the expert, after the gathering of relevant information is critical. Qualification is the process of establishing whether the financial advisor has access to the appropriate financial tools with benefits that will perfectly match the personal circumstances and financial needs of the prospect, giving regard to various factors, including the prospect's budget. It embraces a decision as to whether or not the financial advisor is dealing with the right prospect. This is a stage that can distinguish the true expert from the fake.

Integrity and trust must underpin the financial advising role, and one has to be really wary of who he/she asks for advice from. A good financial advisor is supposed to be your helper, your guide and your teacher in your journey towards your financial goal. Needless to say he/she must have and be seen to have sufficient knowledge in the field of finance and investments, and must be abreast of trends in the financial markets.

There are several tell-tale clues of a sleazy financial advisor. One who has picked up skills from the field and is not certified is very likely to be unprofessional in his/her dealings. The chances are good that securities/shares recommended will be appropriate, if the financial advisor or the company he/she works for is not tied to or is totally independent of the company whose securities/shares are offered. Steer clear of financial advisors who do not spend enough time to get to know what your real financial needs are. Such advisors will come off as wanting to just get the commission they are entitled to in their dealings with you, and not actually interested in helping and guiding you to achieve your financial goal. If you are not the right prospect, a 'true' expert will candidly let you know, hopefully at the qualification stage or otherwise, as soon as it dawns on him/her.

A thorough research into the company the advisor works for will be a step in the right direction. It will be a bonus if you will be chanced to have a chat with some of his/her customers, chosen at random, to assist you to get a feel of the kind of service you may get. Note that it is not just the service you get during the sale or dealings that matters, but more so the after-transaction service.

The financial markets are very dynamic, and it is necessary that one's personal circumstances and financial situation are regularly reviewed by the advisor, and any necessary changes to the financial strategy implemented with ample speed and agility, to guarantee the attainment of financial objectives. A good advisor must progressively add value to the client.

You Might Not be an Investor in the Financial Markets, but a Gambler!

Let me ask you this. Do you think you are an investor? If your answer is 'no', it is wrong, because you are. How do I know that? Because you take risk every split second in your life, even when you are brushing your teeth in the morning, your gum may bleed, but you want your teeth to shine; when you put that piece of potato in your mouth, you can get choked, but you want to satisfy your hunger; even while you are sat there reading this book! You want to assimilate the information, but your eyes may hurt! Each of these activities takes an input or resource, which could be time, money, energy; you name it, that are used in isolation or in combination to achieve an output or result.

An investor is anyone who takes a definite amount of risk, as a result of forgoing a resource (money in the financial markets), in order to obtain a proportionately higher return. Note that when the risk taken is calculated it is known as INVESTMENT; when risk is taken without much thought of the consequence, it is known as GAMBLING. I'd say that as regards day to day activities, you are normally an investor, because you are normally fairly cocksure about the results you will get.

Thus when it comes to making an effort to obtain returns on our principal, we have a choice to gamble or to invest. It is sad to say that a lot of people who consider themselves investors in the financial markets, are realistically speaking, gamblers. If you are somebody already 'directly' involved with the financial markets I have a feeling you are anxious to find out to which category you belong.

Do you practice diversification sufficiently in your investment? Is your strategy for choosing a security/share one based on a long-term study (say ten years or more) of its performance? Do you follow investment fads? Are you quick to sell a security/share you already hold, only to grab a new security that is gaining acceptance in the news, on the back of its high returns? If you answer 'no' to the first two questions, and 'yes' to the rest, the hard truth is you are a gambler. You might not be very bothered about belonging to this grouping now, because you are perhaps young, and have got a lot of money to play around with. Have you really pondered over the kind of retirement you want to have? Have you made sufficient provision for yourself, your lovely children and spouse (if any), in the event of

48

sickness, death and any unwelcome eventualities? Think deeply and earnestly about this.

When it comes to judging performance, the well-being of a security tomorrow cannot be ascertained from its performance today. This is an idea in support of the 'random walk' hypothesis in investment theory. A wise investment hence, will be one in a security/share that has a good past track record; an industry leader for example, with high and reliable returns. Aside of this choice, diversification in the light of industry, and security type (bonds, shares, unit trusts) is also very highly recommended, to increase the chances of guaranteeing the expected returns. There is a massive advantage to be enjoyed from an investment in a unit trust that invests in diverse securities with excellent track record in performance.

Everybody Needs Financial Planning – The Poor Need It The Most!

I am sure you have seen several of those days when at one moment the weather was sunny, and most people you came across wore a nice smile. You were going out with a jumper, but you said to yourself, "Oh what a beautiful day! I don't need a jumper." Then what happened next? You went out, singing heartily to yourself, and when you were far from home, the weather changed all of a sudden. The sky turned sullen grey, you began feeling cold, your hands began to turn into ice, they hurt. This is very typical of the English weather, isn't it?

Interestingly, a lot of us treat our finances just as we deal with the weather. We forget that in life lack has more or less the same chance to exist as abundance. A future worth looking forward to is one that has been to some extent mapped out. Have you ever had the experience of dashing to your room from the kitchen to fetch something, and just on the way having your attention switched briefly to something else, you got into your room and you found yourself for a moment picking something else instead, and then instantly recalling: "Oh no, this is not what I came here for!" That's what you get when you lose focus.

To guarantee the achievement of your short, medium and long-term financial objectives, you don't only have to plan your savings and investments, but you also have to establish and sustain focus. This is because life's circumstances can change really fast, normally without warning, and a well-focused individual will be better placed to identify any changes promptly enough, to effect any necessary changes to financial plans, geared at attaining financial goals.

You may be asking: what have I got to do with investment and savings when I can't even make ends meet? This is normally the excuse of many for not getting involved with anything to do with savings and investments. My wages are not high enough for me to start thinking about investments; they would say. But think about it for a moment, who needs savings and investments the most? The man who is scraping a living or the man who has already made it? It should be the poor man. It is a very sick person who needs to see a doctor to take a prescription for medication. A healthy person probably needs to only by choice take some supplements to help keep him or her in good shape. This is the position occupied by the affluent as regards savings and investments.

The essence of investing is to take a certain amount of risk, with the hope of obtaining some returns on the principal invested. Think about it, it is the one who lacks, who should be under more pressure to gain returns to better his/her social life. It might interest you to know that there are savings/investments like Individual Savings Accounts (ISAs) that have a lot of tax relief benefits and do not need colossal amounts of money to start. Begin now, plan your savings and investments towards a rainy day.

SECTION C: INSURANCE

Know the Features of Insurance Policies

In recent times, there are more indirect investments in the stock market than there are direct ones. Thanks to institutional investors, the private investor has been saved a lot of time choosing and managing his own shares, as well as stockbroker costs which can be a deterrent for some savers. Insurance fund is a major institutional investment which can provide great benefits for the private investor if he will take the trouble to understand their features to know when to use them.

Insurance funds can essentially be divided into three main types: term insurance, whole- of-life insurance and investment bonds. Term insurance and whole-of-life insurance primarily provide life insurance, whereas, investment bonds like the name suggests are investment based.

Term insurance is a temporary policy that insures one for a specific amount and covers a specific period of time. It could range from a period of one week covering death during a holiday to twenty-five years covering a mortgage payment. There are regular premium payments that can be reduced, increased or kept the same, during the term of the policy.

What the investor has to take note of here is that money will only be paid to the beneficiaries of the insured if death occurs within the specified term of the policy. In other words, any money invested will not be paid back to the insured if the term expires and the insured is still alive. This feature of the policy makes it the cheapest insurance policy.

A whole-of-life policy, on the other hand, is permanent and spans the entire life of the individual. There are thus monthly premium payments throughout the life of the insured and automatically comes to an end when death occurs. Unlike term insurance, the insurance company has to definitely pay out money in this policy, and this is a feature that makes this policy expensive. It is also possible to receive cash for the money invested if one turns out not to be able to continue with the premium payments. It is, however, not advisable to use this type of policy as a saving tool due to its costly nature. There are two kinds of whole-of-life policies, namely 'with-profit' and 'without-profit'. A with-profit fund invests in shares, whereas a without-profit one invests in fixed interest securities such as bonds.

An endowment policy combines life insurance with savings. A specific amount is insured, and regular payments are made towards this amount. It is hoped that at a set rate of interest the premiums invested including accumulating interest can be compounded to provide the targeted amount that has been insured at a specified time. If the policyholder dies before the policy is completed, the higher of the value of the premiums plus any accrued interest on the one side, and the targeted amount on the other will be paid to the beneficiaries. The guaranteed amount constitutes the life insurance aspect of the policy.

Endowment policies are suitable for mortgage payments. In this case, interest on the mortgage is paid by the mortgage holder separately from the premium payments. The total amounts of the premium and the interest they accrue go towards paying off the mortgage loan itself at the end of the policy. This type of mortgage payment is different from the repayment type in which each amount paid has a part reducing the loan amount and another part reducing the interest on the loan.

Investment bonds only have a very small life insurance component. They are mainly geared at making returns on investment. There are unit-linked, with-profit, property and money market kinds. The unit-linked kind can be further subdivided into fixed interest, managed, general, and specialist funds.

'Fixed interest' relates to investments in bonds; 'managed' has to do with a much diversified portfolio of shares, bonds, properties and so on; 'general' involves tracking a particular stock index, e.g. FTSE 100; and 'specialist funds' is limited to a specific geographic area or asset class. 'With-profit funds' have to do with unit-trust investment; 'property' funds deal with investment in commercial and industrial properties, and 'money market' funds concern investment in deposits and money market instruments such as CDs and bills.

Life's circumstances change and every situation will merit its own type of insurance. Although insurance funds are useful, the investor must be careful not to place round pegs in square holes or vice versa. Insurance companies are also not all alike, and shopping around before investing will pay high dividends, since for the same type of policy the high-quality companies can guarantee higher long-term payments.

SECTION D: TAX

Learn to Enjoy the Tax Advantages of ISAs

Individual savings accounts (ISAs) provide enormous tax advantages that every investor must try to utilize in a portfolio. There are two main types of ISAs: Cash ISAs and Stock and Shares ISAs.

ISAs have experienced a considerable amount of changes over the years. As from 1 July 2014, Cash ISAs and Stock and Shares ISAs will be combined into a single NISA with a limit of £15,000.

Income tax will not be paid on interest or dividends accrued in ISAs and any profit from ISA investments will be free from capital gains tax.

It makes a lot of sense for every investor to find a place for ISAs in his portfolio. They are ideal tools for reaching short-term objectives, which I suppose every investor has or must have, for example, emergency funds or money to foot car repair bills. The savings on tax payments can go a long way to boost the returns of an investor.

SECTION E: RETIREMENT PLANNING

Will Your Pension Be Enough?

Pension is the amount one receives during retirement as a replacement of the income that was received during one's working life. Pension funds have been in existence for a long time, as institutional investors that help the private investor to amass pension for retirement. A knowledge of the sources of the funds is hereby discussed to help the investor to assess whether enough provision has been made before retirement.

There are broadly speaking two lots of pension schemes: personal and occupational. A personal pension scheme is an individual saving effort made to put aside money towards one's pension during retirement. Occupational pension scheme is associated with the workplace and takes two forms: non-contributory and contributory. A non-contributory pension scheme involves the employer alone paying money into a pension fund towards the retirement of the employee, whereas the contributory kind has to do with the employee also contributing part of his income into the fund.

There are two types of occupational pension schemes: 'defined benefit', also known as 'final salary' and 'defined contribution', also called 'money purchase' scheme. A defined benefit scheme specifies the level of income the employee is entitled to during retirement. The level of income is based on what the final salary of the employee is at the time of retirement, as well as on the length of service in the firm. The money purchase kind does not specify the level of income, but depends on the contribution made by the employee towards the fund, as well as on how well the fund has fared and the annuity rate at the time of retirement.

State pension is always there to provide basic pension, and these other pensions, are to act as supplements. At the time of retirement, the lump sum accumulated in the pension fund for the employee is used to take out an annuity policy in an insurance company, which then ensures that a specified annual amount is paid regularly to the retiree during the entire retirement period.

With the state pension system in a mess it looks like 'defined pension' scheme is what is needed by the employee. The irony is that this type of occupational pension scheme is gradually being wiped out of the system by employers because it is considered very expensive as well as time-consuming. If at the retirement time the pension funds do not perform well enough or the annuity rates are not high enough to provide the level of income guaranteed by the employer in a defined benefit scheme, the employer is supposed to top it up. This is very different from the money purchase kind, in which the employer does not have to bother himself with the performance of the pension fund or level of annuities. It is not surprising that many employers are replacing defined benefit pension schemes with the defined contribution kind, to the detriment of the employee.

It is thus necessary for every employee to find out how much roughly his/her income will be during retirement, relate the figure to the sort of lifestyle anticipated, and if at all the pension will not be sufficient, start stashing some extra money away in a personal pension fund.

Every worker should endeavour to face realities, and not to lose himself/herself in abstraction, when considering pension for retirement. State pension has never been enough and they will never be. It is wise to know how much pension there will be and what is needed as top-up, to ensure an easy and comfortable retirement.

How Much Pension Provision Do You Already Have?

The first step in retirement planning is to ascertain what your financial needs will be at and after retirement. You and your advisor should next proceed to find out how much pension provision you already have. This is important because part or occasionally all of your pension needs would have been already provided for, and you wouldn't want to start saving up for something that already exists; would you? Existing pension provision will fundamentally comprise Basic State Pension and possibly some additional earnings related pensions (top-ups) as well as some occupational or individual pensions. We will consider these in greater depth in the sections that follow.

It is not very straight forward attempting to work out how much state pension you will be entitled to at retirement; only an estimate can be established. Anyone who is more than four months and four days from state retirement age can fill an application form (BR19) and send it off to Department of Works and Pensions (DWP) for a forecast of state pension entitlement.

A State Pension Forecast letter that will be received from the Pension Service of DWP will have a breakdown of how much state pension you can expect in terms of Basic State Pension, Graduated Retirement Benefit, State Earnings Related Pension (SERPS) and State Second Pension (S2P). There will be figures representing the amount of state pension you have earned to date, how much more you might earn between the date of issue and retirement and how much basic state pension you can expect to earn at retirement. The forecast also goes on to suggest possible ways through which the basic state pension can be possibly improved.

The basic state pension forecast is expressed in today's money terms and it does make sense; why? When considering your financial needs at and after retirement, common practice is to express it in terms of a proportion of pre-retirement earnings, which is in today's terms. Since inflation does erode the purchasing power of money, it does make a lot of sense to find out what your pension projections for the future will be (considering inflation) in relation to that proportion of your current earnings (in today's terms). For example the retail price index (RPI) in the UK in October 1983 was 86.7 and 182.6 in October 2003. This means that £1 in 2003 will be needed to buy what 47.5p could buy in 1983.

The forecast will say how many units of Graduated Retirement Pension have been attained and what this is worth. As regards S2P and SERPS it will mention what has been earned to date, what might be earned between the date of issue and retirement, as well as what can be expected at retirement. If there has been any contracting out, the forecast should make mention of what deductions in S2P and SERP it leads to. A widow or divorced person will also get to know possible state pension entitlement that might ensue from the national insurance contributions of the former or late spouse.

If you are an existing member of a final salary scheme, you can find out what pension benefit you have earned in two ways: through the scheme booklet or the annual benefit statement. The scheme booklet will provide you and your advisor information about what the accrual rate of the scheme is (say 1/60th or 1/80th) and also give you an idea of benefits that will be paid on death before or after retirement. With such information you will be able to work out what proportion of your pre-retirement earnings will be paid as pension. Benefits in a final salary scheme of a previous employer will be 'preserved' and revalued annually to the set retirement date. You can also request this benefit to be transferred to a new employer, with a value technically called the 'cash equivalent transfer value'. This is the value of the benefit revalued to the date of normal retirement stated in today's terms. These bits of information put together will enable your financial advisor to find out the value of the final salary scheme benefits at retirement and in today's terms. The annual benefit statement will mention the level of benefit earned to date and your total contributions.

Indeed, the pension provision can also exist in a 'money purchase' scheme which can be an individual pension scheme, such as a personal pension plan, or an employer sponsored arrangement. Apart from Retirement Annuity Contracts, all members of money purchase schemes are entitled to receive annual illustrations known as 'Statutory Money Purchase Illustrations (SMPIs). This illustration does provide an idea of what future benefits can be possibly amassed in the scheme. It provides a pension projection giving regard to the effects of inflation.

The benefit figure is reached by first finding out what benefits have been earned to date, adding future contributions (bearing tax-relief in mind), adding any contracting out rebates, and then subtracting charges and expenses of the scheme membership, as well as expenses relating to risk policies, such as pension term assurance. A growth rate of 7 % is assumed for the illustration, although in order to avoid over-estimation of returns on investment, a figure less than 7 % can be acceptable. The value obtained is then expressed in today's terms, by using an inflation rate of 1.5 %. Finally the fund is translated into pension income by the assumption of an annuity rate. The annuity rate is revalued annually in line with RPI. A monetary value can also be put on preserved benefits to be transferred. It is also possible for your financial advisor to request projections of benefits in future terms, using different growth rates.

Having established your financial needs at and after retirement, as well as how much pension provision there is, the difference between the two constitutes the shortfall (gap), for which a plan has to be put into place to bridge. This will be at a cost which like the other figures should be considered in today's terms. Factors to consider will be inflation, your attitude to investment risk and the charges of the pension contract that will be opted for. Affordability is a big issue, and should be looked at in the light of what your present and future expenditure commitments will be; your other financial priorities such as family protection, mortgage payments, funding children's school fees or going on holiday. You should also consider any anticipated changes in your financial circumstances.

Other financial needs will always exist alongside those of retirement. In fact one's financial needs can be endless, but the bad news is that financial resources are normally very limited. You will hence be duplicating your efforts if you have to put your scarce resources away for what you have already toiled for. Hence the reason why you need to get the figures right as regards what pension provision is already existent and the amount of shortfall that has to be made up. Also remember that pension arrangements are not the only ways of providing for retirement, and the benefits of other investments as options should be compared. The tax advantages of pension schemes should be pondered on, vis-a-vis the added flexibility that other investment options have.

Some Great Questions to Ask During Retirement Planning

You have heard a lot about pensions and the unique tax advantage that is characteristic of them. You have decided to plan for your retirement and have booked an appointment with a financial advisor you trust. There you are on the appointment day sitting in front of your advisor. It is a gorgeous summer's day, with the brilliance of the sun's rays stealing its way through the windowpanes of your advisor's office. A multitude of thoughts pervade your mind, most of which you have managed to block, but one: "I want my days of retirement to be as pleasant as this day – really easy and comfortable." But just how can you ensure the achievement of this end? What sort of questions should be answered, with the assistance of your advisor?

Essentially the process of retirement planning should commence with your advisor establishing what pension provisions you have already, find out what your capital and income needs will be at and after retirement, and ascertain what shortfall exists between your present resources and those needed in the future when you retire. The shortfall should then be quantified in order to be able to plan successfully towards its provision.

Until the right questions are asked and answered it will be impossible to find out what the gap is between your present circumstances and where you want to be at and after retirement. So what are these important questions?

If order is important, I suppose your guess is as good as mine that the first question should be something like: "What provision have you made so far towards your retirement?" In answering this question you should look back, more so if your current employer is not the first. You might have some 'preserved' pension stashed away with some previous employers, and hey don't forget to find out how much state pension you will roughly be entitled to, during retirement.

Now that you know how much pension provision exists, the next important question to ask is, "When and how do you want to retire?" Why is it necessary to know when you want to retire? I know women especially hate talking about their age, more so when it's far from the teens; it is, however, necessary that one gets really open and honest about age at this juncture. A consideration of your age in tandem with when you want to retire will help your advisor to prioritise your needs properly. Prioritisation is important during financial planning because the resources that are available at any point in time will be limited, whereas ones financial needs may be endless! For instance, if you're just in your twenties, with a spouse or civil partner and some children who are financially dependent on you, then protection through say life insurance policies will merit greater attention than savings towards retirement.

When you want to retire has to be known so that with your age in mind your advisor will know how much time you have to save up for the quantified shortfall. But just how would you like to retire? Perhaps you are employed and are considering not retiring outright, but to phase in your retirement by progressively reducing your hours of work over time. Or you might be self-employed or a director of a company and have decided to take less responsibilities over a certain period. Either way, it means that your drawing on your pension will also be phased in. This will reduce the amount of income you will require from your pension, during the early part of your retirement, and should be factored into the retirement plan.

The income and capital needs at and after retirement should also be looked at. Pension schemes pay a tax-free lump sum, currently known as 'pension commencement lump sum'. This lump sum can be used to pay off liabilities or deal with certain capital needs at the start of your retirement, such as paying off the rest of your mortgage, buying a holiday home or indeed replacing a company car.

It must, however, be noted that if the tax-free lump sum is utilised at the start of retirement it will not be available to supplement later income from your pension, implying the need for higher income provision for later years after retirement. On the other hand if you have no plans to use the tax-free lump sum at the commencement of retirement, it will help to reduce the provision that has to be made for income as your retirement progresses.

We have so far been talking about your capital and income needs at and after retirement. One other main purpose of pension arrangement is to ensure that your spouse or civil partner and dependants, such as children are financially catered for should you die.

You have to discuss what the capital and income needs of your dependants will be at and after death. Does your spouse or civil partner have a pension of his or her own? What are the ages of your children and for how long will they need financial support, until they leave home or complete their higher education? Mind you if some of these kids are disabled they probably will need financial assistance for the rest of their lives! Do you have any special retirement plans such as a desire to enjoy a comfortable long-term care?

It is good practice to estimate your income needs after retirement in terms of a proportion of your current salary, of course making allowance for the effects of inflation. Please don't be tempted to say you will need 100 % of your current income as this will be unrealistic and also expensive to provide for.

Remember that in the early years of retirement certain expenses such as the cost of commuting to work will be absent, and mortgage payments would have been completed. On the flip side of the coin, you might want to fund some pastimes and hobbies during the early part of your retirement which may increase your income needs. Later on during retirement the cost of such activities will be reduced only to be replaced by the cost of long-term care and medical expenses. It is advisable, hence, to look at income needs earlier on in retirement in isolation from those of later years.

You will find it rewarding to bear in mind that people are living longer than they used to say, twenty years ago, and this means that annuity rates will be lower and as such more money will have to be saved to provide for the same income than would have been the case in the past. It is hence inadvisable to delay saving towards your retirement as the longer you wait, the more strain saving will have on your income, once you start! As a result of an increase in average life span, if you opt for a final salary scheme, your employer will bear the problem of paying your pension for a longer period; a choice of a defined contribution scheme, however, will place the burden of longer payments on you. If you intend leaving some of your pension fund for your dependants at death, it will influence your advisor's choice of pension arrangement, and you must make him aware of such a desire. Finally, the various questions should be pondered separately as well as collectively as they will be interconnected. For example, your age and how much income you can save will help to answer the question whether or not the date you have set to retire is realistic.

ABOUT THE AUTHOR

In this little book, the author (David Opoku) shares the financial wisdom acquired through several years' practice as a Financial Planning Manager of a reputable international bank in London, and as a financial advisor/stockbroker of another type of Financial Services' institution.

The content of this book will be useful to both the layman who wants to gain greater insight into how to take charge of his/her finances as well as to the seasoned financial advisor, who wants to hone his/her skills in the profession. It will serve as a gem in today's tumultuous financial markets.

Printed in Great Britain
by Amazon.co.uk, Ltd.,
Marston Gate.